365
Days of Prayer
for
Teens

BroadStreet
PUBLISHING

BroadStreet Publishing Group, LLC.
Savage, Minnesota, USA
Broadstreetpublishing.com

365 Days of Prayer for Teens

© 2021 by BroadStreet Publishing®

978-1-4245-6187-2
978-1-4245-6188-9 (eBook)

Prayers composed by Grace Boelter (GB), Abby Erickson (AE),
Aryana Forsberg (AF), Elizabeth Sluka (EHS), Rebecca Sluka (RS),
Cayla Winger (CFW), Chantelle Winger (CGW), and Courtney Winger (CTW).

Designed by Chris Garborg | garborgdesign.com
Edited by Michelle Winger | literallyprecise.com

Printed in China.

21 22 23 24 25 26 27   7 6 5 4 3 2 1

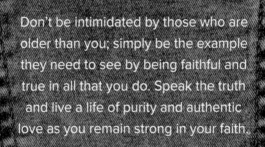

Don't be intimidated by those who are older than you; simply be the example they need to see by being faithful and true in all that you do. Speak the truth and live a life of purity and authentic love as you remain strong in your faith.

1 Timothy 4:12 tpt

Introduction

Whether you have made prayer a habit already or this is your first prayer devotional, inspiration is waiting for you in the daily prayers written here.

Ultimately, prayer is a conversation with God. You don't need to use fancy words or recite long passages of Scripture. Just talk to God. Open your heart to him.

365 Days of Prayer for Teens is a prayer book that will help you connect daily with God. Some days your prayers may be filled with gratitude, others with frustration, and some with need. Lay your heart and your prayers at the Father's feet and wait for his tender response. He adores you, and he's listening to every word you say.

January

Let's not get tired of doing what is good. At just the right time we will reap a harvest of blessing if we don't give up.

GALATIANS 6:9 NLT

A Perfect Plan

Many are the plans in a person's heart,
but it is the LORD's purpose that prevails.
PROVERBS 19:21 NIV

Heavenly Father, as this year begins I am setting new goals and making plans. Both of these things I am doing with expectations of what this year will hold. Each year when I reflect on the past one, it is not my goals or plans that prevail, it is yours. Father, I am thankful that I have no control over what is to come in this new year but that you have full control. I know the story you are writing for me is far better than any story I could ever write for myself.

Help me to set aside selfish desires and seek to understand what you desire for me. Purify my heart. Transform it to be more in sync with your Word. Whatever you have planned for me in this new year, I pray that I would trust you through it all. I know that you will use the hard, the challenging, and the good times in ways far beyond what I can imagine to draw me closer to you. God, help me to lay down every expectation I have of what this year might hold. I give it into your hands so I can lean on you alone to guide me through this new year.

What would you like to see change this year?

Choosing Well

Trust in the LORD with all your heart,
And lean not on your own understanding;
In all your ways acknowledge Him,
And He shall direct your paths.
PROVERBS 3:5-6 NKJV

Father God, you are omniscient and sovereign over all the earth. You have full control over every wave in the ocean and bird in the sky. I know the truth of who you are, yet I continue to rely on my knowledge and understanding to get me through life and I fall short every time. Why do I fail so often to trust you when I see that you have full control over everything in the universe? Why do I let my fears creep in when I know that you hold me?

Help me to commit each day to you, trusting that you will lead me. When my fears and worries start to overwhelm me, I want to seek your wisdom and counsel. It is through your perfect understanding that you guide me. As I trust you with my life, fill my heart with an unexplainable peace that comes from knowing you are in control. When life feels uncertain, you remain certain.

Are you ready to trust God completely with your life?

Work that Matters

Whatever you do, work heartily,
as for the Lord and not for men.
COLOSSIANS 3:23 ESV

God, thank you for renewing my strength each day so I can complete what you have set before me. You are faithful. Teach me to be faithful in all things big and little. Sometimes in life, the small tasks can start to feel so pointless and it is easy to question if they truly matter. When lies and doubts begin to fill my head, remind me that you have a purpose in all things. I want to show up for the everyday realities of life.

Teach me to be faithful in doing the simple and ordinary things well. You use the seemingly insignificant tasks. You use the unseen moments. Father, as I go through life faced with daily tasks, I pray that you would remind me to be faithful because you are a God that uses ordinary things in significant ways. I pray that you would change any self-centered motives I have. Help me live in a way that is not about getting the praise of man, but about bringing glory to you, my creator.

What is your reason for doing all your tasks?

Positive Influence

"Your light must shine before people in such a way that they may see your good works, and glorify your Father who is in heaven."

MATTHEW 5:16 NASB

Heavenly Father, I confess I so frequently fail to live my life in such a way that brings glory to you. I am so incapable of reflecting your heart with my actions, yet it is through empty vessels that you work. Thank you for the ways you meet me in my shortcomings. I am thankful to serve you, a God who takes imperfect people and uses them in your perfect story. You take the broken and make it new.

Father, as I seek to glorify you with my life, I pray that you would continue to point me to your Son, who set a perfect example and loves me with a perfect love. Today I am choosing to believe that in my weakness, your strength is made perfect. In knowing the truth of who you are, I pray that you would use me in ways far beyond what I could ever think to ask. Father shine your light in and through me so that my life may glorify you.

How do your actions reflect the heart of the Father?

AE

Friends Matter

> If either of them falls down,
> one can help the other up.
> But pity anyone who falls
> and has no one to help them up.
> ECCLESIASTES 4:10 NIV

God, you are the giver of every good gift, and I am so grateful for that. As my heart reflects on the endless amount of grace-filled gifts that you have given me, I continue going back to the sweet gift of friendship. Friendship is a beautiful thing. You created people with a need for friendship. I pray that I would not take any friends for granted, knowing that each one is not promised but is a special gift from you. Help me treasure my friendships.

Teach me how to love and care for my friends selflessly, to celebrate them without hesitation in their little wins and their significant victories. Show me how to be there for them on the hard days, not having all answers but pointing them to you, the answer. When the enemy attempts to break apart my friendship with his schemes, I ask that you would protect us. Thank you for providing the precious gift of friends.

Who are your true friends?

Rescue from Trouble

When holy lovers of God cry out
to him with all their hearts,
the Lord will hear them and come to rescue them
from all their troubles.

PSALM 34:17 TPT

Heavenly Father, I come to you today with a weary soul. I am so broken. It is in the brokenness that I feel all the more thankful that I can cry out to you, and you hear my prayers. I am grateful that you do not distance yourself from me during hard times, but you draw even closer. It is such a comfort to know that you not only hear me but also see me and know my heart.

When I face troubles, point me back to your promise that you will never leave me. I am not alone. Through every trial, you are with me. Remind me of the hope that is found in you even when tragic news rocks my world. When I can't do anything but weep. When my heart shatters in a million pieces. There is hope even in the darkest of days. What a blessing and comfort it is to know that you not only want me on my best days, but you want me on my worst. Thank you, Father!

What help do you need from God today?

AE

Abide

"Abide in me, and I in you. As the branch cannot bear fruit by itself,
unless it abides in the vine, neither can you, unless you abide in me."
JOHN 15:4 ESV

Jesus, apart from you, I am nothing. I ask that you would continue to open my eyes to how disparately I need you. Your grace is on display in my life. There are days when I wake up, and I do not want to read your Word. Change my desires. I will starve if I am not feeding myself with your truth. Help me to fight the distractions that hinder me from you. I pray you would give me a new desire each morning that longs to abide in you and your Word.

Father, grow in me godly discipline. Convict me of areas or things in my life that are pulling me away from you. I do not want to be deceived by things that cause my heart to drift from you. Guard my heart. Teach me to value your Word. There are so many people in the world that do not have the privilege of reading the Scriptures; I pray that I would never take it for granted. Instead, teach me to treasure it. Be my all. You are the one true source of life. Thank you for being gracious toward me.

What can you let go of today that keeps you from resting in the knowledge that you are abiding in God?

AE

Fully Committed

"Devote yourselves completely to the LORD our God, walking in
his statutes and keeping his commandments, as at this day."
1 KINGS 8:61 NRSV

Father, this world is full of distractions that fight for my
attention. Daily I consume the ideas of the world. So
many things claim to be worthy of my time and devotion.
In all the noise, I pray that you would keep my eyes
fixed on you. Remove from my life the distractions and
temptations that are keeping me from devoting myself
entirely to you. This life is so short and getting caught up
in doing the wrong things is too easy. Convict me of idols
in my life that I've placed above you.

Father, I do not want to waste my time on things that
have no eternal value. I pray that you would guard me
against being consumed by everything this world has to
offer. Focus my mind on you. You alone deserve my full
devotion. Show me what it looks like to live in devotion
to you completely. Set a fire in my heart that burns with a
deep passion for you. Father, be my everything!

What has been holding you back from being fully
devoted to God?

AC

Deliver Me

"Lead us not into temptation,
but deliver us from the evil one."
MATTHEW 6:13 NIV

Father God, you are my deliverer. You are the source of my hope. You have taken what was impossible and made it possible. It is by your strength alone that I can fight this battle against temptation. As the enemy is continually placing temptation in my life, I pray that you would give me the strength to fight it actively. I do not want to allow sin to have victory in my life. It is so easy to live blind to sin when the world has normalized it and even idolized it.

Father, I pray that you would guard me against being conformed to the world. Protect my heart from the schemes of the enemy. I confess that I have so often made light of my sin. I do not want to be someone who believes the enemy's lies. As I press into your Word, I pray that you would teach me and empower me with truth to fight temptation. As I fight this daily battle against temptation, equip me with strength.

Do you trust that God gives the strength you need to resist temptation?

Accountability

Each one must answer for himself and give
a personal account of his own life before God.
ROMANS 14:12 TPT

Father God, one day I will stand face-to-face with you. On that day, every earthly possession will have absolutely no value. In a moment, everything that this world has placed so much importance on will be nothing. Suddenly the money, the success, the fame, the material items will all be worthless. On that day, when I stand in your presence, the only things that matter are eternal. Did I live my life selfishly trusting myself? Or did I live trusting you and serving others? Did I live seeking to make my name known? Or did I live my life proclaiming yours?

Oh, Father, teach me to live each day with meaning and purpose. I do not want to get to the end and be full of regret because I wasted my life doing all the wrong things. Teach me to value what you value. Give me the boldness I need to share the gospel with the people around me. I pray that I would not waste my life away chasing after fleeting things. In you, there is purpose. In you, there is fullness of life.

What keeps you accountable in your daily life?

So Much Grace

From his fullness we have all received,
grace upon grace.

JOHN 1:16 NRSV

God, who am I that I get to experience your overflowing grace day after day? I am so unworthy of this gift, but in your goodness you continue to pour it out over me. Thank you! You are so good to me. I fall short daily, yet you pursue me still. Help me to accept your grace. It is a gift. I know that I cannot earn it, and I do not deserve it, but in your goodness, you freely give it. Your grace alone is enough to cover me. It is enough to cover my shame. It is enough to cover my guilt. It is enough.

Father, help me to believe that your grace is sufficient, and through it I am made new. I pray that I would live in such a way that reflects the grace I have received. I want to live in freedom, knowing that I am no longer a slave to my sin. Flood every area of my life where I am struggling to allow your grace to pour in. Jesus did not die for some of my sins; he died for all of them. I pray I would believe that with my whole heart and walk in freedom because, in you, I have received grace upon grace.

What areas of your life need God's grace to flood them?

AE

Loneliness

Even if my father and mother abandon me,
the LORD will hold me close.
PSALM 27:10 NLT

Heavenly Father, there are days I feel so alone. Days that I feel forgotten and abandoned. As I walk through life, whether loved ones surround me or not, the days will come when the feeling of loneliness will be very present. When I feel abandoned and when I am hurting, remind me that you hold me. I am not alone. On the days when I feel so forgotten, remind me that my feelings do not define what is true. You are God, and your Word is truth.

When my feelings overwhelm me, I pray that I would cling to you—the source of all peace. Help me find comfort in knowing that you will carry me through every season. You don't need my strength or my striving or my toughness. You just want my heart. I give it all to you in my weakness, trusting that you will be my strength; you will cover me and carry me through. Today I am choosing to embrace my full dependency on you.

How have you seen the Lord's presence in your life?

Refresh and Restore

It is in vain that you rise up early
and go late to rest,
eating the bread of anxious toil;
for he gives to his beloved sleep.

PSALM 127:2 ESV

Lord God, I admit that it is so easy to get lost in the busyness of life. Sometimes it feels like my life is spinning in a thousand different directions, and I lose sight of the one thing that matters—you. Father, in the craziness, teach me to slow down. Teach me to take the time to refresh my soul. Show me how to be still and know that you are God. I want to let go of the things in my life that are hindering me from you.

You did not create me to try to balance everything that life throws at me. No, you created me to be whole, and in you my wholeness is found. No success, achievement, relationship, or career will ever complete me or give me fulfillment in life. You complete me. You are everything that I need. Father, help me rest in you today, knowing that there is fullness of life in you.

What can you do today to establish rest as a ritual and not a luxury?

AE

Fully Sacrificed

I plead with you to give your bodies to God because of all he has done for you. Let them be a living and holy sacrifice—the kind he will find acceptable. This is truly the way to worship him.

ROMANS 12:1 NLT

Heavenly Father, you paid the ultimate sacrifice by sending your Son to die the most brutal death so that I may have eternal life. Oh, Father, I pray that my heart would never grow numb to this reality. I hope to never lose awe in what you have done for me. I want to live in such a way that brings you glory. It's so easy to place my affections, hope, worth, security, and desires into things of this world instead of you.

My body is not my own; it is yours. I want to live in a way that honors you in all aspects of my life. In the way I speak and in the way I act. Help me to live in a way that is not always about me, but instead points people to you. I pray that my life would reflect your character. I am fully known and deeply loved by you. I pray that I would not hold any part of myself from you but instead give you my everything knowing you accept me.

Is there any part of yourself that you are holding back from God?

AÉ

Accepting Others

*As it is in your heart, let it be in mine. Christ accepted you,
so you should accept each other, which will bring glory to God.*
ROMANS 15:7 NCV

Father God, you have accepted me, flawed and unworthy, as your child. Not only have you accepted me, but you have also chosen to love me with your perfect love. Help me to accept others in that same way and do so with a heart of love. I confess that I struggle with this more than I'd like to admit. In my pride, I judge others. I look down upon people who have different sin struggles than my own. I need you to work in me.

It is so easy to get comfortable with loving and accepting the people already in my life. Yet, in doing so, I miss out on opportunities to show your love to others by simply accepting them because you created them. You beautifully designed every human in your image, and I pray that alone would be reason enough for me to love someone regardless of anything else. Take away my pride that blinds me from seeing opportunities to display your love. Humble me. Make me more like you.

Is there someone in your life you have been struggling to accept?

Run to Win

Do you not know that in a race all the runners run, but only one
gets the prize? Run in such a way as to get the prize.
1 CORINTHIANS 9:24 NIV

What a gift it is that I get to look forward to something
far greater than anything this world has to offer, God.
As I run this race of life, I pray that you would keep my
eyes fixed upon what is to come. Life is so fragile and
short. I do not want to waste my time here on earth
getting caught up in things that have no eternal value.
Many things in this world are fleeting. Father, give me an
eternal perspective. Use my life to show the world what
Jesus has done. Use my life to make your name known
and to bring you glory.

I want to live in such a way that reflects that I genuinely
believe that the best is yet to come. The trials and the
suffering I experience in this life will not compare to the
glory that is to come. Help me cling to your promises and
live in hope because the best truly is yet to come.

Are you caught up in the cares of the present, or are you
living with the end in view?

AE

Forgiven

"Whenever you stand praying, forgive, if you have anything against anyone; so that your Father in heaven may also forgive you your trespasses."

MARK 11:25 NRSV

Heavenly Father, thank you for sending your Son to die so I might be forgiven. I am so undeserving of your forgiveness, but in your love and perfect grace, you have given it to me. Forgiveness is an area of my life that I so desperately need your help with. It is one of the hardest realities on earth. Apart from you, I am unable to do it. Continually point me back to the cross when my heart is struggling to forgive. When I let bitterness creep in, remind me of what you have done for me. I want to forgive without hesitation because that is what you have done.

Father, help me not only to forgive with my words but also in my heart. Wipe away the pain others have caused me. Give me the grace to love. You do not just forgive me. You choose to remember my sins no more. Help me to choose forgiveness over bitterness so I experience the freedom that is found in giving all of my pain to you and trusting you to heal me.

Who can you forgive today?

Always Thankful

Give thanks in all circumstances;
for this is the will of God in Christ Jesus for you.
1 THESSALONIANS 5:18 ESV

God, I am thankful for your steadfastness. Through the storms of life, you remain faithful. I embrace your never-changing character. Living in a world where things are constantly changing, my heart is so grateful to serve a God who stays the same. Thank you for the ways you love me unconditionally. Thank you for spreading your goodness over my life. You are worthy of all my praise. In the darkest of days, still you are worthy of my praise because you remain good.

Father, when my mind shifts from what I don't have or what I can't do, move me toward thankfulness. There is a purpose for every trial, every failure, and every heartbreak. I don't always see how you use every challenge for good, but that is okay. You are God. I am not. I have to trust you. Teach me to be thankful in all circumstances knowing that I have a good Father. Thank you for being patient with me as my heart learns to find contentment and gratitude in every season.

Can you practice gratitude in the challenges in your life?

AE

Inspire Me

God created great sea creatures and every living thing that
scurries and swarms in the water, and every sort of bird—
each producing offspring of the same kind.
And God saw that it was good.

GENESIS 1:21 NLT

Heavenly Father, you are the creator of life! You created
every good and perfect thing You made every star in
every galaxy, and you know each one by name. I marvel
at all that you've created! You paint every sunrise and
sunset, each one beautifully different. I am in awe of who
you are. You are the Creator of all things, and you know
my name. Not only do you know my name, but you know
every detail about me. What a precious reality!

As the whole world displays your beauty, God, I pray that
I would not get lost in scrolling on my phone, searching
for inspiration. I want to find my inspiration in you and
what you've created. What you have to offer is so much
more than what the world offers. Help me to let go of
the distractions that are stopping me from living in the
fullness of Jesus. Inspire me with the beautiful world and
the fantastic creatures that you have made.

Where do you find inspiration?

No Compromise

"If you love me,
obey my commandments."
JOHN 14:15 NLT

Jesus, I admit that I speak of my love for you so often, yet my actions do not reflect my words. I lack faithful obedience to your Word. Help me grow in godly discipline so I may live a more fruitful life. As I read your Word, convict me of areas in my life that do not agree with it. Reveal to me ways that I have misinterpreted it.

Father, I pray that I would never read your Word and interpret it in a way that makes me feel best, but that I would seek to understand its true meaning. Help me to be someone who not only reads the Bible but who also strives to live out what it teaches. As I seek to obey your commandments, teach me to wrestle well and dig deep so I may gain not only knowledge of it but understanding. I love you, and I pray that my life would grow to reflect that.

Have you grown lax in following Jesus' instructions for life?

So Tired

Those who wait for the LORD shall renew their strength,
they shall mount up with wings like eagles,
they shall run and not be weary,
they shall walk and not faint.
ISAIAH 40:31 NRSV

Heavenly Father, I come to you today, tired of trying to do everything in my own strength. I am weak. I am weary. Life gets busy. Sometimes I start running a hundred miles an hour trying to keep up with everything, and I can't catch a breath. I forget to step back from the craziness and take a moment to breathe. To breathe and say thank you. And to slow down and wait for you.

You are the source of all my strength. Every breath in my lungs and beat of my heart is from you. Thank you for giving me another day of life. Each moment is a precious gift. In the chaos, you are faithful. In my weakness, I am trusting that you will be my strength. You will continue to carry me through. I am thankful that I can come to you, and you give me rest. I pray that you would continue to renew me each day.

When you are weary, where do you turn for strength?

AE

Season of Grief

Since we believe that Jesus died and rose again, even so, through Jesus, God will bring with him those who have fallen asleep.

1 THESSALONIANS 4:14 ESV

Father God, when I am suffering, you are still good. When I am stunned by grief, in every trial, in even the most painful situation, you are good. Help me to believe that with my whole heart. I do not understand why you allow certain things to happen the way they do. But I just have to trust. It is in the seasons of grief that I long even more for the day that I will be with you—the day when there will be no more tears, no more pain, and no more grief. You hold my tomorrow.

Father, help me to trust you with today, knowing that you will be faithful moment by moment. I cling to the hope that you keep your promises. You are trustworthy. You are faithful. Father, I pray that when I go through seasons of grief, I would come out on the other side more like you, closer to you, more dependent on you, and with more awareness of you. You are with me through it all, on every mountain top and in every valley.

When grief sweeps into your life, how do you deal with it?

Loving Well

"I am giving you a new commandment, that you love one another; just as I have loved you, that you also love one another."

JOHN 13:34 NASB

God, your love is unconditional. It never fails. It is patient and kind. It is selfless. You love me so well! I pray that you would help me love others. Teach me to love with your love. Show me areas of my heart where I struggle to love. I'll be the first to admit that it is a constant battle to fight against my selfishness. I fail to love others above myself. Cleanse me from my selfish ways. Please continue to pour out your grace over me.

On the days when loving others feels impossible, please point me back to the cross. Remind me of your staggering love for me. Your love is so great and costly. Father, I pray that as I seek to love others they would feel your love through me. I want the world to know that you are a loving Father, that while they were still sinners, Christ died for them. I pray that my life would reflect just a small glimpse of your abundant love.

How can you choose love that prefers others over your own interests?

AJ

Casting Burdens

Cast your burden on the LORD,
And He shall sustain you;
He shall never permit the righteous to be moved.

PSALM 55:22 NKJV

Heavenly Father, I come to you today with a heavy heart. I confess that I struggle to cast my burdens on you. I have pride in my heart that convinces me that "I've got this," but the truth is, I don't! I am weak. My burdens are heavy. I can only carry so much weight until I am crushed by it. I am so grateful that you, my loving Father, don't want me to carry the weight of my burdens, but instead, you desire me to cast them on you.

Father, I pray that you would help me to cast all of my burdens on you. You have the strength to carry the weight. You have the power to overcome every obstacle. Teach me to let go of doing it on my own and let you carry the heaviness. I pray that I would surrender to you today every burden that is weighing me down with confidence that your mighty power will take them.

What are you weighed down by?
Can you give your burdens to the Lord today?

Mercy upon Mercy

"They are blessed who show mercy to others,
for God will show mercy to them."
MATTHEW 5:7 NCV

Father God, you have shown me mercy time and time
again. I mess up, fall short, and sin against you, and still
you continue to forgive me. Thank you for the mercy you
have shown me. Thank you for giving me freedom where
it is so undeserved. Because of your mercy, I am no
longer bound to my shame. Help me to show that same
mercy to others.

Father, keep me from seeking out vengeance. That
belongs to you alone. Too often, I place myself in your
role and try to bring justice to situations that I do not have
the authority to rule over. You are a God of justice. I trust
that you will bring perfect justice. Teach me to be merciful
because that is what you ask of me. Father, when I am
wronged or hurt by someone, I pray that by your grace,
I would show mercy. Help me to live a life that displays
your mercy.

Have you been holding onto a grudge?
How can you extend mercy instead?

AE

Quick to Listen

Take note of this: Everyone should be quick to listen,
slow to speak and slow to become angry.
JAMES 1:19 NIV

Lord, you are so patient with me. You continuously pursue me even when my heart wanders from you. You hear my cries for help. You are infinitely wiser than me, yet you listen to my every thought. Father, I want to be more like you. I am quick to speak my mind instead of listening to the hearts of others. Help me become more compassionate and kind. Teach me to slow down and listen and not be quick with anger. I need you.

My words can come so fast. Thank you for being gracious toward me. Help me be gracious toward others. You are patient with me in my imperfections. Give me patience. I pray that each day you will continue to mold me into your likeness. Take what is broken in me and remake me to be more like you. Father, I ask that you would help me listen with love and speak with your heart and not a quick temper.

Are you quicker to speak or to listen?

Forever Gifts

When God chooses someone and graciously imparts gifts to him,
they are never rescinded.

ROMANS 11:29 TPT

God, thank you for the talents, gifts, and abilities you
have given me. I confess that it is easy for me to overlook
those gifts. I see the gifts you have given others and
the way they use them to serve and glorify you, and I
question why I wasn't given what they were. I make up
excuses and tell myself that if only I had what they had, I
would be content. But Father, it's a lie because you have
graciously given me my own unique set of gifts to equip
me for what you planned for my life.

Father, open my eyes to see the value in the gifts that
you have given me so I may use them to their fullest
potential. Take any jealously or comparison in my heart
that is robbing me of living out the life you have for me.
Shift my heart from envying others to being encouraged
by them. I pray that when I see people using the beautiful
gift you have chosen for them for your glory, I would get
excited. Turn my mindset from competition to opportunity
to serve together with your people.

What are some of the gifts that God has given you?

While I Wait

Be strong, and let your heart take courage,
all you who wait for the LORD!
PSALM 31:24 ESV

Heavenly Father, I confess that there are days I feel like you have forgotten me. I wait, yet it feels as though nothing happens. I know your promises, but my heart and mind fight to understand. In my wondering, doubting, aching, longing, and grieving, fix my eyes upon Jesus, the perfecter of my faith. Fix my eyes on truth. You have a plan. You have a purpose, even in the waiting. When I get so caught up in my plans, I forget that your timing does not have to fit my timetable. Your ways are not my ways.

Father, remind me that you are omniscient, your plan is perfect, and you have much better timing for every part of my life. You waste absolutely nothing. You are limitless in your ways, and you work in every season. Waiting is tough, but there is so much hope because you promise victory over all things. Death is defeated. It is finished. There is hope! Fill me with your courage and your strength even as I wait.

What encourages you in times of waiting?

AE

Every Good Thing

Every good thing given and every perfect gift is from above, coming down from the Father of lights, with whom there is no variation or shifting shadow.

JAMES 1:17 NASB

Lord, I am so undeserving of everything you have given me. Today you continue to pour out your goodness over my life. I have so much to give thanks for, yet my heart is frequently discontent. Oh Father, give me eyes to see your goodness in my life and a heart that is content. I pray that you alone would be enough to satisfy my soul. Regardless of my circumstances I pray that I would give you thanks because no matter what my life looks like, the goodness of the gospel remains true. My debt has been paid. My sins have been washed away.

Father, let that be enough. I pray that I would rise each morning and give you praise because you have given me the gift of salvation and that alone is worthy of all my praise. You have filled my life with an abundance of gifts, giving me reason upon reason to give you glory and honor. Thank you for the ways you have blessed me. I can't say thank you enough. You are so good to me!

What good gifts do you see in your life?

AE

Confession of Faith

If you confess with your mouth the Lord Jesus and believe in your heart that God has raised Him from the dead, you will be saved. For with the heart one believes unto righteousness, and with the mouth confession is made unto salvation.

ROMANS 10: 9-10 NKJV

Father God, thank you for salvation through the Jesus! Please give me boldness to confess my faith openly to the world without fear. Help my faith to be strengthened and my relationship with you to grow deeper. Faith is not always comfortable, and it is not easy. Grant me your strength. As I live for you, I pray you would daily refresh my heart with love for you. Help me to represent you through the way I live in the big and little things. I want to choose you in the day-to-day.

Lord, give me a willingness to sacrifice earthy things because I have hope in something far more significant. I pray that you would protect my heart from doubts or unbelief that creep into my life. I come to you today broken but overflowing with joy and hope because one day, I will be made new. I cling to your promises. You are my strength. You are my joy. You are my hope.

How does your confession of faith shape how you live your life?

Gentleness

Remind the people to be subject to rulers and authorities,
to be obedient, to be ready to do whatever is good,
to slander no one, to be peaceable and considerate,
and always to be gentle toward everyone.
TITUS 3:1-2 NIV

God, even though my character may sometimes change quickly, yours never does, for you are consistent and unchanging. I know that you value obedience, thoughtfulness, and gentleness, so I give you full control over my mind, will, and emotions. I want my thoughts and actions to reflect who you are, so come be at the center of all my relationships.

Jesus, I invite you into my interactions with others so they may be peaceable. Help me to be considerate of others and demonstrate gentleness even when it may be hard to do so. Guard my heart against all bitterness and annoyance so I am able to love others well. When there is a situation where it is hard for me to love someone, I ask that you would show me your thoughts and perspective. I want to reflect your heart toward everyone around me.

Does your life reflect the radical way of love?

RS

February

The temptations in your life are no different from what others experience. And God is faithful. He will not allow the temptation to be more than you can stand. When you are tempted, he will show you a way out so that you can endure.

1 CORINTHIANS 10:13 NLT

First Stone

When they persisted in asking Him, He straightened up
and said to them, "He who is without sin among you,
let him be the first to throw a stone at her."
JOHN 8:7 NASB

Father, you delight in showing mercy and at the same time upholding justice. I am in no way perfect, yet you desire to have a relationship with me and always show me kindness. Although I am not deserving of your love, you sent your Son, Jesus, to die for me and take away all the sins of the world. I surrender to you any shame or guilt I have due to my sins, so I am able to live out the fullness of my salvation.

I invite you to convict me of the ways I have not shown mercy to others as you have shown to me. Help me be compassionate toward those around me even if they have wronged me and are not deserving. Rid me of all pride in my heart so I am able to empathize with others, forgive them as you do, and live a life of purity.

What stones have you been ready to hurl at others that you can lay down today?

RS

All I Need

My God will supply every need of yours
according to his riches in glory in Christ Jesus.
PHILIPPIANS 4:19 ESV

God, you are my provider. You are abundant in your
blessings and plentiful in gifts. Forgive me for the ways
I have not allowed you to provide for me, like thinking I
could do things on my own. I surrender and want to lean
on you for all my needs, for I know you will never let me
down. I trust that you will take care of me no matter what.

Guard me against being blinded by the riches of this
world; I want you alone to be my security. I give up any
fears or false expectations I have about my needs, and I
choose to look to you. You are sufficient for me. I praise
you for all the ways you have provided for me, and I am
open to receive all that you have in store. I need you, I
want you, I choose you, and I trust you.

How have you seen God provide in your life?

Humble Rescue

I've learned from my experience
that God protects the childlike and humble ones.
For I was broken and brought low,
but he answered me and came to my rescue!

PSALM 116:6 TPT

God, you are my protector and rescuer. I know that you will never force yourself upon anyone, so I humbly ask for your intervention in my life. I am thankful that I don't have to strive to be heard by you and that you are always faithful to answer when I call. Although I may not feel it, I know your presence is always near me, for you hold me in your hands and care for me unlike anyone else.

Father, help me to be childlike and accept your guidance and healing hand in my life. Come heal all of my brokenness. Even though I've tried to fill it with many different things, now I know that only you can fill the emptiness in my life. When I feel hopeless, afraid, broken, alone, or confused, I trust that you will be my help on the way. I submit to your protection and rely on you to be my rescuer.

How can you practice being humble today?

RS

Power Supply

He gives power to the faint,
and strengthens the powerless.
ISAIAH 40:29 NRSV

God, you are the all-powerful king of kings. Your power is greater than any other, and nothing is able to stand against you. With your power alone, you can cure diseases, break addictions, and soften the hardest of hearts. Thank you that, with the Holy Spirit, I may also manifest your power. I open my heart to his guidance and strength, and I give you complete lordship over my life. I receive and claim the authority you have given me as your child.

I know that in my weakness, you remain strong, so help me look to you for strength to overcome any scheme of the enemy. Train me up so I can be a vessel for you and your kingdom. Help me showcase your power through my life so others may come to see your greatness as well. May everything I do be unto giving you glory.

What weakness can you invite God's strength into today?

RS

No Small Miracle

You are the God who performs miracles;
you display your power among the peoples.

PSALM 77:14 NIV

Father God, you are the miracle worker. I am so captivated by everything you do. Even the breath in my lungs was a miracle made possible by your incredible creativity and power. You are always working for good and your actions display your righteousness. You are able to intervene and radically change the toughest of situations and circumstances. I am in awe and amazed by your works! You cause the blind to see, broken bones to heal, and the dead to come alive.

I cannot believe that I am loved by you, the King of glory. You do with ease what everyone else considers impossible. Remind me of all the ways you have displayed your mighty works in my life so I may praise you for them. Help strengthen my faith so I partner with you and also perform miracles in your name. Make me aware of how you are working today.

If you think about the impossible being done, when was the last time you saw or heard of a miracle?

RS

Inspired to Please

"Be careful! When you do good things, don't do them in front of people to be seen by them. If you do that, you will have no reward from your Father in heaven."

MATTHEW 6:1 NCV

God, you are all-seeing and all-knowing. You see me in the secret place and know everything I think, say, and do. I invite you to sit on the throne of my heart. I want to stop living for the praise and reassurance of others. Help me live my life as a sweet, pleasing gift unto you. Help me to not be like the Pharisees who acted like they knew and loved you but were hypocrites. I want to truly know your full nature and character.

Father, I ask that you would expand my capacity to sit with you and have a daily lifestyle of prayer. Grant me the grace to put you above all else and stand against anything that may try to inhibit me from coming humbly before you each day. You alone are worthy of all praise and worship. Thank you for always being available and for showing up whenever I seek you.

If you look at the way you live your life, both privately and publicly, do you see a difference between the attitude of your heart in those moments?

RS

Confidence

Do not throw away your confidence,
which has a great reward.
HEBREWS 10:35 NCV

God, I choose to put my confidence in you. Help me come before your throne with confidence, so I may receive mercy and find grace to help me whenever I am in need. Thank you for making a way for me to be in your presence and for fighting my battles. You give me such freedom and joy knowing that you hear me whenever I ask anything according to your will.

Reveal to me all the ways that I have thrown away my confidence by putting it in other things. I ask that you would forgive me for them. I choose now to put my trust in you. I know that I have great confidence through Christ and that it is better than anything else in this world. Help me to remain by your side all the days of my life as you have been at mine. I choose to lock eyes with you.

What are you most confident about?

RS

Remain Faithful

If we are faithless, he remains faithful—
for he cannot deny himself.
2 TIMOTHY 2:13 ESV

Father, thank you for your faithfulness. You are reliable in all circumstances and meet my every need. I praise you because you always keep your promises and you are faithful even when I am faithless. Remind me today that I need not worry; rather, I can simply remain in you. You know all that I need even before I ask, and you desire for me to live abundantly.

Forgive me for the ways I have doubted you or fallen short of your will for my life. Show me how to behold you and walk with you, so I can resemble more of your likeness each day. I want to be steadfast in loving you like you do me. Soften my heart and direct me toward your ways. Remind me of how you have been faithful to me so I can worship you in a way that you are worthy of.

How has God's faithfulness changed your life?

RS

Diligence Matters

Be diligent in these matters; give yourself wholly to them,
so that everyone may see your progress.
1 TIMOTHY 4:15 NIV

Lord, I know you see all my hard work and accomplishments. Forgive me of all the ways I have not stewarded well what you have given to me. I now want to offer all that I have to you for your glory. Train me to be diligent and use the gifts you have given me to their full potential. May I show the same diligence as the saints who have gone before me with full assurance of hope unto the very end.

Through it all, help me listen and abide in you instead of striving. Thank you for continuing to be steadfast and ministering to me even when I may not fully deserve it. I want to be faith-filled and trustworthy so I may inherit all your promises for me. It's my desire to give myself wholly to you and to do only the things that you lead me to.

How do you react to change?

RS

Right Obedience

Peter and the apostles replied,
"We must obey God rather than any human."
ACTS 5:29 NLT

Father God, I thank you that you are a good leader. It is my joy to live in your will. I ask that you would open my ears so I can hear your voice more clearly and obey. Your direction in my life is better than anything I could receive from the world, so help me put your instructions for me above all others. Help me follow you unconditionally and with no excuses.

You never lead me astray, so I know I can trust your leadership and be quick to obey you. Forgive me for any ways that I have disobeyed you. I want to live my life fully unto you, not just partially. Help my "yes" mean yes and my "no" mean no. I know that your ways are so much better than mine, so I invite you to do your will in my life. I choose to live a life of simple obedience.

What does it mean for you to obey God today?

RS

Become New

If anyone is in Christ, there is a new creation:
everything old has passed away;
see, everything has become new!
2 CORINTHIANS 5:17 NRSV

Thank you for sending your Son to die for my sins, God. You have paid a price that has delivered me from my slavery to sin. I believe in you and receive your forgiveness. I am no longer a slave to fear, doubt, worry, hatred, anger, lust, pride, or anything else that leads to death. Now, I am a child of yours. I have been bought, redeemed, set free, clothed in garments of righteousness, and seated with you in heavenly places!

As your child, help me to walk in my new identity. Help me see you fully so I can know who I really am in you and keep my eyes forever on yours. May your love compel me to live for you and not myself. Thank you for drawing me near to you. Help me never stray from your presence. I am a new creation. The old has gone and the new has come.

What areas of your life need a new touch from God?

RS

Content in All

I know what it is to be in need, and I know what it is to have plenty. I have learned the secret of being content in any and every situation, whether well fed or hungry, whether living in plenty or in want.

PHILIPPIANS 4:12 NIV

Lord God, you are my rock. I thank you that you are not circumstantial and that your character never wavers. Help me grow my faith in you so that when hard times come, I can stand firm in you. Show me more of who you are, so I have greater confidence in your character and leadership in my life. Help me realize that the safest and most satisfying place for me to be is where you are no matter the circumstance.

Jesus, align my priorities so I am able to embrace all that you have for me even if it may seem crazy in the world's eyes. Forgive me for any ways I have taken you for granted. I don't want to just have you when times are either good or bad, so help me stay constant in my pursuit of you. You are worthy of all my attention regardless of my situation.

Does your belief about God and how he sees you change when your circumstances shift?

RS

Let You In

Search me, O God, and know my heart;
test me and know my anxious thoughts.
PSALM 139:23 NLT

Father, I know that you know me inside and out, including all my thoughts and worries. I invite you to break down any wall that I may have put up to isolate myself and hide my feelings. Help me to be vulnerable with you, for you are the one true comforter and friend. Help me always run to you for help before seeking it somewhere else.

I pray against all the lies that I have believed about myself, you, and others. Come renew my mind so all my thoughts become yours, and I experience true rest in you. Let your peace wash over me like a river, giving me a sound heart and mind. Remind me that I do not have to always come to you put together, but that you love me in my brokenness. I choose to let you know me and renew my heart and thoughts.

Can you give God control of your thoughts today, inviting him into that space, to bring peace to worries and anxiety?

RS

You Are Love

He who does not love does not know God,
for God is love.
1 JOHN 4:8 NKJV

God, you are love. Your love is one that surpasses all others. When I am fixed on your love, all other lovers fall away, for yours is never-ending and the only one that can truly satisfy. Thank you for unconditionally loving me although I am not deserving. Because you gave the ultimate demonstration of true love by sending Jesus to die for me, I choose to live my life loving you in return. Help me build my life on the foundation of your love.

There is no limit to the amount of love I can receive from you, so I ask that you would come and consume my life with it. Guide my thoughts and actions so they reflect your love in every situation of my life. I want to be forever captivated by your love and marked as one who loves as Jesus did. Your love is more than enough.

Where do you see the thread of God's love?

RS

One Heart

"I will give them one heart, and put a new spirit within them.
And I will remove the heart of stone from their flesh
and give them a heart of flesh."

EZEKIEL 11:19 NASB

Lord God, thank you for your renewal. Although there have been many times I have distanced myself from you, you never fail to bring me back and restore what has been broken. You are a jealous God, so I ask you to forgive me for having other idols in my life that have been placed before you. I give you full permission to come and take back first place in my heart.

Help me be fully devoted to you and not distracted or wooed by the things of this world. No evil can reside amidst your holiness, so help me live a lifestyle of being set apart for you. Help me behold only what is considered right in your eyes so that my life produces good fruit. Thank you that, by your grace, you have put a new spirit within me to help me walk in purity and holiness.

What difference do you see in your heart as you walk with God?

RS

Every Opportunity

Don't allow yourselves to be weary or disheartened in planting good seeds, for the season of reaping the wonderful harvest you've planted is coming!

GALATIANS 6:9 TPT

God, you are perfect in your timing. I am grateful that I get to live in this generation. I know that you have a plan for my life. I want to be a part of your great commission, so send me out and use me to make you known. Help me make the most of every opportunity while walking in obedience to the Holy Spirit. Guide me and speak through me when I share your good news with others.

I ask that you would break off all fear of man so that I am able to boldly proclaim your gospel. Let me not grow weary or lose heart if I do not see any results because I know you will cause every seed sown to bear lasting fruit in your timing. Help me walk with you and abide in you all the days of my life. Thank you for making me a partner and friend to work with in your harvest field.

What opportunities do you have to show the character of God to others?

RS

Given Completely

Submit therefore to God.
But resist the devil,
and he will flee from you.

JAMES 4:7 NASB

God, you are trustworthy. I know I can trust you with my life, so help me live completely surrendered to you. I ask for you to awaken a deeper longing in me for greater intimacy with you. Break all limitations I may have thought there were for how much I could know you. I invite you to come with your presence and invade every part of my life. Forgive me for the ways that I have withheld from you. Help me to recognize and turn away from all that which hinders the growth of my relationship with you.

I want my life to reflect full devotion to you, Father. Thank you that, through Jesus, you have given me authority over the enemy. When the wicked pry or evil temptations come my way, help me rebuke them and turn to you. Thank you for always being with me and for giving me the tools to resist the enemy.

How has fear kept you from giving yourself completely to God?

RS

Anger Rising

"In your anger do not sin":
Do not let the sun go down while you are still angry.
EPHESIANS 4:26 NIV

Help me live out my life righteously, Lord. Although it is not a sin to be angry, for even Jesus had moments of being righteous in anger, it is important how I choose to act upon it. Help me to not have a quick temper when I feel angry, but to control it and release it to you. You are just, so I know I can trust you to make all wrongs right in the end. Keep me from suppressing anger or harboring it away because that only turns into bitterness.

Forgive me of the ways that I have let my anger control me. I invite you to break down any walls I have built up in my heart due to anger, fear, pain, bitterness, or hatred. You do not keep records of my sins, so help me let go and forgive those who have wronged me. Remind me to always act out of love.

How do you react when you get angry?

RS

Measured Steps

We also pray that you will be strengthened with all his glorious power so you will have all the endurance and patience you need.
COLOSSIANS 1:11 NLT

Heavenly Father, true rest is only found in you. Even though it is not bad to be busy, it can get in the way of my quiet times with you. Help me realign my priorities so that my first becomes intentionally spending time with you. Strengthen me during that time so I have all the endurance and patience I need for each day.

Help me find joy in doing things with you and in giving you worship. Minister to my heart and give me deeper revelations about yours. Forgive me for all the times I have not put you first or listened to your commandment to rest. I know that your commandments are best for me. Help me find my rest in you because all offers of peace outside of you are only temporary. Help me keep my eyes on you, even during busy seasons of life.

How can you make space in your life for intentional rest?

RS

Pursued by Goodness

Why would I fear the future?
For your goodness and love pursue me all the days of my life.
Then afterward, when my life is through,
I'll return to your glorious presence to be forever with you!
PSALM 23:6 TPT

Father, thank you for your goodness and that you never stop pursuing me. I praise you because you are always near and always good. No matter the future, I can have assurance that you are with me. Your goodness is overwhelming. I am so thankful for who you are. I ask that you reveal your goodness to me in a new way, so I may be able to give glory back to you by honoring others with godly kindness and love.

Even when I walk through painful and difficult situations, thank you for continuing to be near me. Thank you for the blessed assurance that you care about me and are constantly thinking about me. I am so excited to be with you forever. I want to pursue you like you pursue me. Remind me of your goodness today and for the rest of my life. I praise your name.

What was the last thing God did that gave you assurance that he was with you?

Separated from Guilt

Since we have been justified by faith,
we have peace with God through our Lord Jesus Christ.
ROMANS 5:1 ESV

God, sometimes I let my guilt get in the way of my relationship with you because I am afraid you are angry with me. Thank you for declaring me in right standing with you. When I make mistakes, you call me back to you with the same amount of love as if I had never done anything wrong. I am free to run to you for help and comfort no matter what. I don't deserve it, which makes your love so much more incredible.

Thank you for separating me from my guilt so I can live without any shame. Thank you for seeing me for who I am in Jesus and not how the world sees me. I ask that you show me any aspects of my life that I have been withholding from you because of guilt. I want to give those to you and freely receive your peace through your Son, Jesus Christ. Being justified by faith is the greatest gift! I cannot praise you enough

Is there guilt you've been feeling about your relationship with God that you can let go of today?

EHS

Not Afraid

In God, whose word I praise,
In God I have put my trust;
I shall not be afraid.
What can mere mortals do to me?

PSALM 56:4 NASB

When I am afraid, Father, I try to hold onto my situations and do everything myself. Sometimes I just freak out instead of crying out to you for help. The truth is, with you, I don't need to fear anything. You hold me and the rest of the universe in your hands with ease. You know everything and you have power over everything. I don't need to fear what comes next; you are right beside me always.

Your will is perfect, and what you have planned is better than anything I could ever think of myself. I don't need to fear others because nothing they do can separate me from you. Help me to cast my fears at the cross and trust in you completely. I don't want to have anything in my life that holds me back from trusting in you. Even when enemies surround me, you are there protecting me. Fear, go in the name of Jesus!

What fear has been holding you back from fully trusting God?

EHS

Restraint

"Put your sword back in its place," Jesus said to him, "for all who draw the sword will die by the sword. Do you think I cannot call on my Father, and he will at once put at my disposal more than twelve legions of angels."

MATTHEW 26:52-53 NIV

God, some situations make me so angry that I want to lash out or retaliate. Sometimes I see injustice or unfairness and want to take matters into my own hands. Give me the ability to step back and listen to what you want rather than do what I think is right. Your ways are better than my ways, and I want to be in alignment with your plans in every situation.

Thank you for your endless patience and for your timing that is perfect. Show me when to speak out and when to stay silent, when to act and when to wait. I want to do good works for your glory. I ask that you reveal any actions I am taking, even apparently "good" things, that are contrary to what you want for the situation. Please make me more like you in this part of my life.

Are you trying to do for God, through force, what he could do on his own but chooses not to?

EHS

Move Me

When He saw the multitudes, He was moved with compassion
for them, because they were weary and scattered,
like sheep having no shepherd.

MATTHEW 9:36 NKJV

Father, thank you for always having time for your children. I can come to you no matter the day or hour, and you are willing and ready to listen. You are so compassionate, even to those no one else pays attention to. The busyness of life can make me forget to stop and think about others. I ask that you help me reorder my priorities, so I take time to be compassionate.

Sometimes I bypass situations because I don't want to have to deal with feelings or with being uncomfortable. Not knowing what to do makes me want to forget all about it. I repent for all the times I have ignored your whispers that tell me to pause and look. I want to have your perspective on life; show me what you see in others and give me your heart for them. Show me how to be as compassionate as you are.

Can you make space in your day to allow God to move your heart in compassion where you would normally brush past it?

EHS

What Really Matters

I want you to understand what really matters, so that you may live pure and blameless lives until the day of Christ's return.

PHILIPPIANS 1:10 NLT

Lord, sometimes I am so wrapped up in my own head that I lose sight of what is really important. Schoolwork, friendships, and what's going on in the world constantly captivates my attention. I repent for letting even good things supersede my focus on you. Thank you for making it clear in your Word what is important in life and how to pursue it. I want to live blamelessly in your eyes and bring you glory with everything I do.

Reveal to me the parts of my life that should be pruned so I am best able to be fruitful for your kingdom. Help me surrender things that I have been holding back for whatever reason, whether it be fear, stubbornness, or my desire to control my surroundings. Reveal to me your divine priority list and what really matters in life. I am so thankful that you know all things. I am forever amazed by your great perfection.

What can you surrender to God today?

Sit and Wait

Wait for the LORD;
be strong, and let your heart take courage;
wait for the LORD!
PSALM 27:14 NRSV

Father God, waiting can be so frustrating! Sometimes I wait so long that I feel like your promises will never happen. But I'm thankful that you are the ultimate promise keeper, and your timing is perfect. I ask that you develop a habit of patience in me even when I don't see the point in waiting. I want to be able to sit and wait on you earnestly, like Mary did at Jesus's feet.

Help me get the most I can out of periods of waiting and seek you even more despite not knowing the future. Thank you for the privilege of being able to seek you in the first place. Reveal to me how amazing of an opportunity it is to wait on you while I am here on earth. I praise you because you know what's best for me. Give me the strength to look expectantly to the future without missing out on what you're doing right now.

How have you seen God move for others who have waited on his promises?

EHS

Releasing Kindness

"Love your enemies, and do good, and lend, expecting nothing in return, and your reward will be great, and you will be sons of the Most High, for he is kind to the ungrateful and the evil."

LUKE 6:35 ESV

Lord, I'd like to think I'm a kind person, but I know that I tend to only be kind to people I like. It's hard to be kind when I think someone doesn't deserve it. It's so much easier to be rude or passive aggressive when others bother me. How amazing it is that you don't do that at all! I can be the most incompetent person in the world and you'll still show such love and kindness. Who am I to say whether someone deserves kindness? *I'm* not deserving, but you care about me unconditionally!

Thank you for loving me when I treated you like my enemy. Help me care for others as precious creations instead of according to standards that I or anyone else puts on them. I want to be a vessel of your love no matter who I interact with. Soften my heart so I can be intentionally and genuinely caring to everyone especially people I don't get along with.

Who can you be intentionally kind to today?

EHS

Saturated in Prayer

Don't be pulled in different directions or worried about a thing. Be saturated in prayer throughout each day, offering your faith-filled requests before God with overflowing gratitude. Tell him every detail of your life, then God's wonderful peace that transcends human understanding, will make the answers known to you through Jesus Christ.

PHILIPPIANS 4:6-7 TPT

God, with you in control, I don't need to be anxious about anything. Worry, be gone in the name of Jesus! I don't want to waste time worrying anymore. Help me come to you first when a problem arises in life before I even have time to be anxious about it. I ask that you change my mindset and help me cultivate a consistent habit of prayer. I want to talk to you about everything because you are the one who has power over every situation.

Thank you for the peace that you gladly bestow on me whenever I come to you with worries. I ask that you continue to guard my heart against any attack of fear and anxiety so I run to you with all my thoughts and requests. I can't praise you enough for who you are. Worry has no hold on me!

What areas of worry can you offer to God in prayer today?

EHS

March

Don't be afraid,
for I am with you.
Don't be discouraged,
for I am your God.

ISAIAH 41:10 NLT

New Life

Anyone who belongs to Christ has become a new person.
The old life is gone; a new life has begun!
2 Corinthians 5:17 NLT

Lord God, thank you that I have become a new creation in you! The moment I gave my life to you, you took my brokenness and turned it into something beautiful. Thank you that I am not only a new person once. You continually guide my heart to seek you and follow you even after my new life has begun.

God, I know I am not perfect. I know there will be moments in time when I am reminded of my old life. In these moments, please help me run to you. Even when I feel stuck, you are right there encouraging me. Even in my hardest times, you still love me. Thank you for never giving up on me. I thank you that your mercies are new every morning. I want to live my new life for you. Please give me the strength to follow your commands and lean on your Word for wisdom.

Are there areas you have felt stuck in that you want to see change?

CTW

Fear Not

Fear not, for I am with you;
be not dismayed, for I am your God;
I will strengthen you, I will help you,
I will uphold you with my righteous right hand.

ISAIAH 41:10 ESV

Lord, there are times when I feel so afraid. Sometimes I have smaller fears about what I will wear, but sometimes I have really big fears about my future. Your Word says I should not be afraid because you are with me. You tell me not to be dismayed or worried because you are my God. I know you hold my life in your hands. Help me to remember that I have nothing to fear because you hold me near.

Father, when I am afraid, I do not feel strong. Your Word says you will strengthen me and help me. Please help me release my fears to you and be strengthened by who you are. The Bible tells me that you will uphold me with your righteous right hand. Thank you that you continue to hold me up. Instead of just lifting me once or twice when I am afraid, you will hold me continually. I release my fears to you today.

What fear can you give to God today?

CTW

Faith Spilling Over

"Whatever you ask in prayer believing,
you will receive it all."
MATTHEW 21:22 NASB

Father, sometimes when I ask you for something, I do not have faith that you will answer my prayer. Sometimes I doubt that you are listening to me. In your Word, you tell me you hear me, and you answer me. Help me to believe that you will answer every prayer no matter how big or small it is. When I pray, I will have faith and believe that I will receive what I have been asking for.

Lord, help me to remember that you can answer my prayers in a different way than I expected. You have what is best in mind for every person on the earth including me. Sometimes I am hurt because a negative thing happened even though I had been praying really hard about it. Please help me to remember that you are a good Father who I can trust and depend on.

What can you ask for in faith today?

CTW

A Place for Me

"There are many rooms in my Father's house; I would not tell you this if it were not true. I am going there to prepare a place for you."

JOHN 14:2 NCV

Lord, I know that everything you put your hand to reflects your character. You are always welcoming and open. Thank you for building a house that mirrors who you are. A house with many rooms that will always let me in. I know I never need to be restless or worried because I know where I will live forever. That place is with you in heaven. Your Word tells me this is true.

Father, thank you that you not only provide a place for me, but you prepare it specifically for me. You design the room to fit me, the person you've uniquely created me to be. Father help me to believe that there is a place for me in your eternal kingdom. I may not know where I belong on earth, but I feel hope rising in my heart as I know where I belong forever. I belong with you, in your eternal kingdom. I can feel your perfect peace falling over me.

Do you believe there is a place for you in God's eternal kingdom?

CTW

My Mistakes

Though he fall, he shall not be cast headlong,
for the LORD upholds his hand.
PSALM 37:24 ESV

Lord, I thank you that you uphold me when I fall. You prevent me from falling completely. Please remind me of this in the moments I feel weakest, in those moments where I feel like I can't get up. Thank you for your unfailing grace that helps me stay firmly planted even when the wind blows and knocks me down. You gently come alongside me, and you lift me up.

God, I thank you that my strength comes from you and you alone. While I may be able to lean on my own strength for a time, I can't always hold myself up. In those moments I feel weakest, you are my strength. There will never be a day where you are not strong enough to lift me up. There will never be a mistake too big that you turn away from me. Thank you for continually grabbing hold of my hand and lifting me up.

Do you believe that you are defined by your mistakes or by God's great love for you?

CTW

If I Wander

> "If a man has a hundred sheep but one of the sheep gets lost, he will leave the other ninety-nine on the hill and go to look for the lost sheep."
> MATTHEW 18:12 NCV

Father, just as a man searches to find his one lost sheep, you seek after me when I am lost. You will even leave your other ninety-nine sheep just to find me. In the midst of every storm and hard situation, you will never stop searching after my heart. Even if you have to climb mountains or dig holes deep into the ground to find me, you will never stop. Thank you for pursuing me even when I forget or choose not to pursue you.

Lord, help me to remember that no matter what sin I have committed, you will continue to find and rescue me. When you find me, you do not yell at me or tell me how bad I am. You always welcome me into your open arms. You call me your child. You are such a good father. Thank you for always chasing after me when I wander.

Do you trust that the Lord sees you when you wander and that he will rescue you?

CTW

My Strength

I can do all this through him who gives me strength.
PHILIPPIANS 4:13 NIV

Lord, today I feel tired. I feel overwhelmed. There are so many tasks I need to complete. I tried leaning on my own strength, but it is not enough to keep me going. Sometimes I try leaning on my parents' strength because they seem much stronger than me. But sometimes they are not strong enough to carry me and themselves. Your Word says I can do all things through you because you give me strength. Your Word does not say I can do all things through my parents' strength.

Lord, I need your strength to fill me. God, you know what I need strength for. Today, I ask that you would fill my body, heart, and mind with your strength. I pray that your strength would not only be enough to complete what I have to do today, but to fulfill me for the whole week, month, and even the year. In each moment I feel weak, help me to cry out to you to be my strength.

What do you turn to when you are tired and worn out?

Deepest Desire

"You will seek Me and find Me when you search for Me with all your heart."
JEREMIAH 29:13 NASB

God, the more I seek after you, the more I will find you. Sometimes I try to seek you, but I don't seek you with my whole heart. I get distracted in my time with you. My mind fills with thoughts that are not centered on you. I think about my homework or my friendships or my plans for tonight. Make my heart steadfast for you. Give me the desire to earnestly seek you with my whole heart.

Lord, I pray my gaze would be fixed on you just as your gaze is fixed on me. Help me to search after you in the same way you seek after me. I want to find you. I want to learn more about your character and what you think of me. You say that I will find you when I search for you with my whole heart. Please give me the strength and joy to search after you that way.

Do you spend more time thinking about what you need from God or about getting to know who he is?

CTW

Child of the King

The Father has loved us so much that we are called children of God. And we really are his children. The reason the people in the world do not know us is that they have not known him.

1 JOHN 3:1 NCV

Father, thank you for calling me your child. You are the most patient, kind, trustworthy, and good father in all the world. My heart is filled with joy because I know I am a part of your family and your kingdom forever. In you I have found my identity. Help me to approach you as my father. I don't want to hold back when asking you for help. You know my heart and I thank you that I do not have to hide anything from you.

God, today I pray you would turn people's hearts toward you. I want them to know you. I want them to know they are children of the most loving, caring, and good father. I ask that you would use me as a vessel of your truth to speak to those who do not know you as a father. As much as I need you, they need you too.

How do you approach God?
Do you know he is your good Father?

CTW

My Help

I look up to the mountains and hills, longing for God's help.
But then I realize that our true help and protection
come only from the Lord,
our Creator who made the heavens and the earth.
PSALM 121:1-2 TPT

God, I'm tired of trying to help myself. I feel drained and overwhelmed, as though my control over my life is slipping through my fingers. I long for your help and your strength. I know it is only you who can truly help and protect me. God, if you made the heavens and the earth, how much more do you want to help me? If you protect the heavens and the earth, how much more would you protect me?

Please take control of my life. I know since you created me, you know how to best help my messy life fall into a beautiful place. I know it may not be easy to give you control, but I know it is what is best for me. Father, I declare that you have control over my life. Do with it what you will. I know your plans are best.

When was the last time you asked for help?

CTW

Drawing Me Back

May the Lord of peace himself give you peace at all times in every way. The Lord be with you all.

2 THESSALONIANS 3:16 NIV

Lord, I thank you that you are the Lord of peace. Not only do you give peace to your children, but you created peace and you reign over it. God, your Word says that you give peace at all times in every way. This means that in the little or big situations, I can ask you for peace and you will give it to me. Sometimes I am restless when I lay in bed at night. In those moments, I can ask you for peace. Sometimes I am anxious when I have a test. In that moment, I can ask you for peace.

God, thank you that no matter what time it is or what I am doing, I can ask you for peace if I do not feel like I have it. Thank you for being with me at all times of the day. I ask that right now, your peace would wash over my heart, my mind, and my body. I pray that throughout this day or as I lay my head down to sleep, you would surround me with your peace and comfort.

What does the fruit of peace look like in your life?

CTW

Though I Fail

My flesh and my heart may fail,
but God is the strength of my heart
and my portion forever.
PSALM 73:26 NIV

Lord, I know there have been times in my life when my flesh and my heart have failed you. Sometimes, my heart has been angry with someone. Sometimes, I have made choices based on the pleasure my flesh receives, rather than making choices that are pleasing to you. Lord, I know there will be times in the future where my flesh and heart will fail. I thank you that you are the strength of my heart forever.

You have always been the strength of my heart and you will forever be. Your Word says that you are my portion forever. God, this means you are always going to be more than enough for me. I will never run out of your grace or love. Your strength will never fade. Please continue to give me grace when I stumble. Help me to remember how you see me regardless of when I fall. Thank you for never giving up on me.

Does God think differently of you when you fail or when you succeed?

CTW

Running Over

"Give, and you will receive. You will be given much. Pressed down, shaken together, and running over, it will spill into your lap. The way you give to others is the way God will give to you."

LUKE 6:38 NCV

Lord, help me to be more generous with what you have given me. There are times where I can be so selfish even though you have given me much. I thank you that when we give, you give even more to us. You give us so much that it spills over into our laps even when it is pressed and shaken together. You are a good, generous God. I want to be more like you.

Today, I want to start being more generous with what I have. Your Word says that the amount I give to others will be given back to me in even greater measure. I do not want to give to others only so I will receive more. I want to give to others with no selfish ambition in my heart. I want what I give to be pure and of you. Please help me as I decide what I can be more generous with. Move my heart in the way you want to.

What can you be generous with today?

CTW

Laying Down Weapons

"The LORD will fight for you,
and you shall hold your peace."
EXODUS 14:14 NKJV

Lord, recently I have been fighting my own battles. Sometimes I feel embarrassed that little things in my day cause me to become worried and not at peace. I try to fight the battle on my own instead of asking for your help. The Bible says you fight for me so that I may hold my peace. I have noticed when I try to fight my own battle, I am still worried and anxious. I cannot fight my battles and still hold my peace.

God, I know you can do this. In this moment, I give my battles to you. From the smallest to the biggest, I declare that I am laying my weapons down so you take over and fight for me. As you fight for me, I feel less anxious and worried because I know that you will always win the battle. You have never lost a battle, and you never will. Thank you for fighting for me so I can hold my peace.

Have you been fighting a battle that is wearing you down?

CTW

The Sweetest Fruit

The fruit of the Spirit is love, joy, peace, forbearance,
kindness, goodness, faithfulness, gentleness and self-control.
Against such things there is no law.
GALATIANS 5:22-23 NIV

Lord, I thank you for all the fruit of the Spirit that you so
freely give to me. When I need more of one fruit—whether
it be kindness, self-control, or a different one—you tell me
I can reach out and take it. There is no law that says I can
only have one fruit at a time. There is no law against how
much of one fruit I can take. You say that I can take all of
them when I need them.

Today God, help me to search my heart and find which
fruit I need more of. Was I loving toward myself or
those around me today? Was I gentle with my words or
thoughts today? You know which fruit I need more of. You
know my heart better than I do. Please help me to take
freely of the fruit you have provided. As I take of the fruit
you have given, I will declare your praises and bless your
name for all you have given. Thank you, Lord!

What fruit do you need more of in your life today?

CTW

Break My Heart

He was amazed to see that no one intervened to help the oppressed. So he himself stepped in to save them with his strong arm, and his justice sustained him.

ISAIAH 59:16 NLT

Lord, I pray this verse would reflect me and my actions. I pray that as I see someone who is oppressed or pushed down, I would step in and help them. Maybe it is someone at school who is teased or maybe it is someone I see who is sad when I am walking through my neighborhood. I pray that your wisdom would come to me when I look around and see who I can help or be a friend to.

I pray I would step out in boldness to be a light to those around me. My arms may not be very strong but with you by my side, I am strong. I pray you would open my eyes to see those around me who need you. Use me to bring your truth to people. I want to serve you and the people around me.

When was the last time you felt fierce compassion for someone?

CTW

Your Motives

Am I now seeking the approval of man, or of God? Or am I trying to please man? If I were still trying to please man, I would not be a servant of Christ.

GALATIANS 1:10 ESV

Father, I am sorry for the many times I have sought the approval of man before I sought after you. Your Word says that when I try to please man, I am not being a servant of you. I want to be your servant not a servant to man. I want to please my Father in heaven, the Lord of all creation, the one who created me.

God, please help me to always seek to please you. In this moment, help me to search my heart honestly. Whose approval am I seeking? Am I seeking approval from my parents about what I do in my free time? Am I seeking approval from my friends about the clothes I wear? Am I seeking approval from my coach about how I played the game? Lord, I repent of the times I have sought after man's approval instead of yours. Thank you for forgiving me. How can I please you today?

Who are you living to please?

CTW

Live with Purpose

The LORD has made everything for its purpose,
even the wicked for the day of trouble.
PROVERBS 16:4 ESV

Father, sometimes I feel like I have no purpose. There are some days where I feel like I do not serve you or the people around me. Yet, you still declare that I have a purpose. I pray I would not let the days just pass by me. I pray that each day, I would live my life according to your purpose for it.

Jesus, I want to wake up each day ready to serve you and go to bed each night praising your name. Sometimes I do not know what my purpose is. Right now, I pray you would give me wisdom to see it. I pray you would speak to my heart and mind about how I can serve you with my life. I thank you that I am young and I have so much time to find my purpose. Please help me to use my time wisely to seek after your kingdom and your heart.

Where do you find purpose in your life?

CTW

Before I Speak

To watch over mouth and tongue
is to keep out of trouble.
PROVERBS 21:23 NRSV

Lord, I confess there have been many times where I have spoken poorly about another person. I have used words I am not proud of. In your Word, you say to watch over my mouth and tongue is to keep out of trouble. When I have spoken poorly about something or someone, it never is good. I either get into more trouble, or I feel guilty.

Lord, I need your help to watch the words that come out of my mouth. I pray that before I speak, I would think about what I am saying and if it is a good thought or if it would hurt someone. I know this is going to take time and I may stumble. In the times when I stumble, please help me to seek forgiveness from you and from the people I spoke negatively with. Thank you for always forgiving me and for helping me when I fail. I want to be more like you. I know I can do this by pausing to think about what I say before I speak.

Do you pause to think about what you're saying about others when they're not around?

CTW

What Is True

It is the greatest joy of my life to hear that my children are consistently living their lives in the ways of truth!

3 JOHN 1:4 TPT

Lord, I repent for the times I have not lived my life according to your truth. Your Word is filled with important values about how I should live to honor you. I pray you would teach me these values as I search for them in your Word. Speak your truth over me. When I stumble, I pray you would remind me of the truth in how I should live.

You say it is the greatest joy of your life when I consistently live my life in the ways of truth. I want to bring you joy. I want you to be delighted in me. I do not want to sometimes live my life in the way of truth. I want to consistently do it. While I know it may be hard, please continue to guide my path and provide me with grace.

What values define the way you live?

CTW

Light of Approval

Indeed, by faith our ancestors received approval.

HEBREWS 11:2 NRSV

Father, I thank you that I do not have to earn your approval. You have looked at me with approval in your eyes since the day you created me. I am thankful that my works do not make you love me more or less. The only way I can receive the approval I am looking for is by faith. Faith is not a work that I have to complete; it is a decision I make to trust and believe in your promises.

I want to have faith like my ancestors. I want to have faith like Esther as she trusted you to speak to the king. I want to have faith like David as he trusted you to defeat Goliath. Please give me the faith and courage to believe that I do not have to earn your approval. Help me to know you love me and have accepted me into your kingdom.

Are you trying to earn God's approval?

CTW

Whatever the Circumstance

I am not saying this because I am in need,
for I have learned to be content whatever the circumstances.
PHILIPPIANS 4:11 NIV

Father, there have been many times where I am not content with where I am in life or what I am doing. Sometimes I am not content when I have to do the dishes. When I go through a tough season—maybe a ruined friendship or even the loss of a loved one—I am not content. But I want to learn how to be content no matter the circumstance I am in. I do not only want to be content when everything is going right in my life because I know more often there are difficulties than easiness.

Today, I choose joy. I choose to be content because my circumstance may not be able to change, but my outlook of the situation can. In every situation you were in, you remained constant and content. I want to be more like you. Help me to be content in every situation I face. Help me to find joy even when I am in seasons of need.

Does your contentment change based on your circumstances?

CTW

Saved from Fear

I asked the LORD for help, and he answered me.
He saved me from all that I feared.

PSALM 34:4 NCV

God, sometimes I am paralyzed by my own fear. I am afraid of disappointing my parents, failing in school, or ruining my relationships with my friends. I do not want to live in a place of fear anymore. Your Word reminds me that you save me from all that I fear when I ask for your help. I need your help. I declare in this moment that I believe your peace will fall on me. I tell fear to be removed from my mind as I trust in you and your unfailing love.

In this moment, I turn off any doubt that you cannot hear me or that you will not answer me. You say when I ask you for help, you will answer me. Thank you for answering my cries. I know you are never going to let me down. Continue to renew my mind and fill me with confidence in who you are: a father who loves me and desires to rescue me.

What fears are keeping you from moving forward today?

CTW

Your Will

"Your kingdom come.
Your will be done,
On earth as it is in heaven."
MATTHEW 6:10 NASB

Father, I know I have tried to live my life according to my own will. I know there have been times where I chose what I wanted to do not what you would want me to do. I am sorry for the times I have hidden from you or not listened to what you have spoken to me. I know you have built heaven to be the most incredible place in all of creation. If you designed a place like that, I want your will to be done on earth just as it is in heaven.

God, I give you control of the plans I have for my life. I know you may support the plans I have now, or you may radically change them. Give me the obedience to remain faithful to you even if you change my plans. You tell me multiple times in your Word that you know what is best for me. Help me to believe this and trust you to guide me in your purpose for my life.

Is there room in your life for God to change your plans?

CTW

Not Helpless

When the righteous cry for help, the LORD hears
and delivers them out of all their troubles.
PSALM 34:17 ESV

Lord, I thank you that I am not helpless. Some days, I feel helpless on my own, but with you I am never completely helpless. When I am in need, I can cry out to you. You will not only hear me, but you will deliver me from my trouble as well. Your Word says you will deliver me from not just one or two troubles, but from all of them.

Jesus, today I need you. I ask that you would wash my heart and make me righteous before you. Your Word says you hear and deliver the righteous. Please make my heart pure and clean before you. Come and rescue me; I am crying out for your help. Meet me today. I know you hear me. You know my every need and see all of my troubles. Thank you that you will not only deliver me from one of them; you will deliver me from all of them.

What help do you need today?

CTW

With Joy

Rejoice in the Lord always;
again I will say, rejoice!
PHILIPPIANS 4:4 NASB

Jesus, you are so good! Right now, I lift my joys to you. From my greatest to my smallest, I lift them up to you. Thank you for providing many joys in my life. Sometimes it is so much easier to see the troubles and negativity in my life. Right now, I ask that you would fill my mind with all of the joys in my life. I thank you for everything you have given me and everything you have in store for my life. I thank you that I have found my identity in you as your beloved child.

Father, as I rejoice in the present joy, I ask that you would pour greater joy into my life. I pray joy would overflow from my heart and begin filling the hearts of those around me who may not know you. You are so good to me.

What joys are in your life right now?

CTW

Surrendered Mind

To set the mind on the flesh is death,
but to set the mind on the Spirit is life and peace.
ROMANS 8:6 NRSV

Father, I am sorry for the times I have set my mind on my flesh—on worldly things—rather than on you. I have noticed when I set my mind on the flesh, I am never satisfied. I always want more and more. Sometimes, I set my mind on getting a new pair of shoes. Once I get them, I am happy for a time, but then I notice a new pair someone else has, and I set my mind on getting those. In these moments, I am never at peace. My mind is always seeking after the next best thing.

Lord, in the moments I seek after my flesh, my thoughts about others do not reflect you. I am more jealous, angry, and ungrateful. When I set my eyes on you, I feel peaceful. Rather than worrying about worldly ideas and items, I can focus my attention on what really matters—you. I pray you would renew my mind today. Help me to center my attention on your Spirit so I find life and peace.

How often do you notice the nature of what your thoughts reflect?

CTW

Repentance Matters

*"Repent of your sins and turn to God,
for the Kingdom of Heaven is near."*
MATTHEW 3:2 NLT

Father, I know there have been many times I have hesitated from repenting of my sins because I feel ashamed and unworthy of connecting with you. When I do this, it pushes me further from you. I want to be closer to you. Right now, I repent of my sins. I repent of being unloving toward others and searching for pleasure in idols that are not you. Thank you for always forgiving my sins, washing me clean, and making me pure.

Lord, your Word says the kingdom of heaven is near. I know my time here on earth is short compared to eternity. Father help me to remain kingdom focused. I want my mind, body, and heart to please you all the days of my life. I want to be a pure and spotless bride before you, and I know the only way to achieve that is by repenting of my sins and turning to you.

Is there something that is keeping you from connecting with God?

CTW

Tempted

Let no one say when he is tempted,
"I am tempted by God";
for God cannot be tempted by evil,
nor does He Himself tempt anyone.
JAMES 1:13 NKJV

God, sometimes I place the blame of temptation on others rather than on myself. It feels easier to blame others for the temptation I feel because I don't want to take responsibility or I am ashamed. I pray that I would acknowledge my temptation and turn from it. This verse reminds me that you never tempt me.

Jesus, you can't be tempted by evil. As I try to be more like you, I pray that I would also not be tempted by evil. I pray that my eyes would be fixed on your gaze and that I would be seen as righteous in my thoughts and actions. On the day you return, I want to be a spotless bride before you. When I feel temptation coming upon me, help me to resist it by turning to you or others who can encourage and build me up in your truth.

When you are tempted, what can help you resist it?

CTW

Not My Home

Stop imitating the ideals and opinions of the culture around you, but be inwardly transformed by the Holy Spirit through a total reformation of how you think. This will empower you to discern God's will as you live a beautiful life, satisfying and perfect in his eyes.

ROMANS 12:2 TPT

God, it is easy to get caught up in the idols and opinions of the world around me. I do not want to live my life according to man or my own flesh. In this moment, I pray you would begin transforming my heart to seek only after your kingdom. I pray my eyes and ears would be open and sensitive to your Holy Spirit.

Lord, I want to know your will for my life. I want my life to be beautiful, satisfying, and perfect to you. I know this can only happen when my heart and mind are transformed to think with heavenly thoughts and values. As this month is coming to an end, I want to reset my priorities. I want you to be first. Each day I live, I want to have listened to your Holy Spirit and to have lived according to your will. Lord, I ask for grace as I learn how to reset my priorities.

When you consider how short this life is, how does that make you rethink your priorities?

CTW

Selfish Ambition

"Whoever exalts himself will be humbled,
and whoever humbles himself will be exalted."

MATTHEW 23:12 ESV

God, help me to humble myself before you. In the moments where I feel entitled and capable of doing things in my own strength, break me to realize I am nothing without you. In the moments where I feel like my own timing is correct, show me that your ways are perfect and the best.

Help me not to get in the way of the beautiful things you have set in place for me. I am weak in many areas, but where I am weak you are strong. I ask for your strength to be humble so my life glorifies you.

Is getting your way more important than unity with God and others?

April

How can a young person
live a pure life?
By obeying your word.

PSALM 119:9 NCV

No Criticism

Keep a good conscience so that in the thing in which you are slandered, those who disparage your good behavior in Christ will be put to shame.

1 PETER 3:16 NASB

God, I pray that I will stand strong in my faith and in my relationship with you. Give me the strength to be bold and fearless when it comes to speaking your name. The world can be harmful and pressure me to keep my mouth closed. It can make me feel ashamed of my personal relationship with you.

I pray you give me the strength and courage to speak of you and the glorious miracles you have done in my life. You are glorious, Lord, and I am grateful for your love and affection.

How do you react to criticism about your relationship with God?

Prone to Wander

LORD, I know that people's lives are not their own;
it is not for them to direct their steps.
JEREMIAH 10:23 NIV

God, I fully surrender myself to you now. I give you my thoughts, my future goals, my job—my life. You have control over it all. I do not want to direct my own path, for I know that will fail. I know that what you have in store for me is beautiful, and I want to fulfill the plan and calling you have placed on my life.

Everything you have created is good and has its own purpose. I don't want my life to be mine, so I surrender it to you now. Direct my steps, so I know I am on the right path moving in the right direction.

When you feel far from where you think you should be, what gives you hope?

The Perfect Way

As for God, His way is perfect;
The word of the LORD is proven;
He is a shield to all who trust in Him.

PSALM 18:30 NKJV

Lord, thank you for knowing what is best for me even when I don't see it. I know and believe that everything you put me through is for a reason and serves a purpose. I thank you for all the situations and events that you have allowed me to go through to help benefit and develop my character.

Your ways are the best and I make room for you to do whatever you want to do. Please provide me with the strength to continue to have an open heart to you. I know your way is perfect because you have proven over and over that it is. You will be my shield as I trust in you.

What are the best attributes you have seen God exhibit in your life?

Source of Hope

I pray that God, the source of hope, will fill you completely with joy and peace because you trust in him. Then you will overflow with confident hope through the power of the Holy Spirit.

ROMANS 15:13 NLT

God, I need your peace in this moment. I run to you with arms open wide knowing that no one else will fully give me the comfort and care that I need. I truly want to be filled with your never-ending love and Holy Spirit. I know you will always provide a safe place for me, and I should never have doubts about that.

I pray against the enemy's attack or anything that wants to come against me. I pray that they would not make me think differently of your mercy and continuous love for me. I want to be filled with confident hope through your Spirit.

What are you hoping for today?

Desiring Humility

The reward for humility and fear of the LORD
is riches and honor and life.

PROVERBS 22:4 ESV

Lord, I know I am nothing without you. I am human and know I will always fail if I rely on myself, and that will never change. You have created me to be on this earth for a plan and a purpose, and I am created to lean on you through every circumstance.

I never want to experience anything without you. Nothing matters more than fulfilling the plan you have for only me to complete. I will fall and stumble, but I know you will continue to be by my side regardless of how incomplete and faulted I am. I am forever grateful for your gift of honor and life in spite of my weakness.

What does submission to God, in humility, look like to you?

Cannot Be Lost

Every valley shall be raised up,
every mountain and hill made low;
the rough ground shall become level,
the rugged places a plain.

ISAIAH 40:4 NIV

Lord, you see me. You see me as an individual and you know my name, my story, and my future. You have always seen me even when I don't feel visible to my friends or family. I thank you that you have been present through the good and bad circumstances in my life.

I am eternally thankful that I never have to doubt your presence in my life. If I only rely on my friends and family, I know they will never come close to the comfort and reassurance that you give me. Your presence is eternal. You work within my situations to create a safe place for me. You are my provider and protector.

Do you believe God is with you in your life right now?

Renew My Mind

Let the Spirit renew your thoughts and attitudes.
EPHESIANS 4:23 NLT

God, I want to represent you well. It is so easy for me to act selfishly and fall into my own stubborn ways. I need to always remember that I have people watching me even when I don't think they are. My actions, my attitudes, my thoughts, and my intentions all need to be checked. I want to represent you well when I am with other people. I want my actions to glorify you and my thoughts to align with yours.

You, Lord, are worthy of all of me. Please provide me with people who keep me accountable and have the boldness to call me out when I am not acting the way I should. Allow my heart to be open and receive their input, for I know they speak with love. Help me to be submitted to your Holy Spirit so my thoughts and attitudes are renewed with your perspective.

What thoughts and attitudes reflect the character of God?

Be You

Since we have gifts that differ according to the grace given to us,
each of us is to use them properly.

ROMANS 12:6 NASB

Lord, I thank you for the gifts you have blessed me with.
I thank you that you have designed them specifically
for me and for the purpose you have for me. It is so
remarkable to see different gifts through different people
being lived out. Every person you have created is unique
and serves a special purpose. I thank you that where one
person is weak, another is strong.

Father, you have planted specific gifts in each individual
that you will use to impact their life and the lives of
others. I pray that I would use the gifts you have blessed
me with to their full potential. I don't want to use them for
myself but to impact and bless others. I know this is what
you want me to do, so I be confident that you will bless
my offering.

What are you good at doing that doesn't come as easily
to others?

Wise Enough

If any of you is lacking in wisdom, ask God, who gives to all
generously and ungrudgingly, and it will be given you.
JAMES 1:5 NRSV

God, I want to receive the wisdom you have. I know that
you can give it to me in full, and that is what I need. I
want to have your insight and wisdom with every choice
I decide to make. I am grateful that you have placed
friends and family members in my life who know about
your wisdom. I know that you use them to speak to me. I
pray that I will listen to what they say and take it to heart.

Father, I truly want to receive your wisdom because I
know I will be much more successful if I do. Thank you
that you will give generously as I continue to ask.

Where do you need God's wisdom in your life right now?

Willing Submission

Obey your leaders and act under their authority. They are
watching over you, because they are responsible for your souls.
Obey them so that they will do this work with joy, not sadness.
It will not help you to make their work hard.

HEBREWS 13:17 NCV

God, help me to respect the leaders you have set in my
life. You have placed certain people in my life for events
and situations to pour out wisdom that will help guide
me. Please give me the ears to hear their words and the
obedience to respond. I want to strongly consider what
they share with me.

I am human, and I stumble and fall. You are watching out
for me and, even when I can't see it, you have placed
leaders and elders in my life to speak your words and
directions to me. I want to listen and receive with an
open heart.

Who can you submit to rather than fight against today?

Self-Discipline

As for us, we have all of these great witnesses who encircle us like clouds. So we must let go of every wound that has pierced us and the sin we so easily fall into. Then we will be able to run life's marathon race with passion and determination, for the path has been already marked out before us.

HEBREWS 12:1 TPT

Lord, give me the strength to let go. Provide me with the willingness to forgive others who have wronged me and help me to forgive myself. I pray you give me the courage to give you all my ties and weights that are holding me down in this time and season. I know they are holding me back from the purpose you have before me.

God, I pray that my heart will not be tough and stubborn, but I will give everything to you. I want to fulfil the calling you have for me, so help me release the wrongs and sins so I can run with passion and determination.

What do you need to let go of today?

Real Future

Come now, you who say, "Today or tomorrow we will go to such and such a town and spend a year there, doing business and making money." Yet you do not even know what tomorrow will bring. What is your life? For you are a mist that appears for a little while and then vanishes. Instead you ought to say, "If the Lord wishes, we will live and do this or that."

JAMES 4:13-15 NRSV

Lord, I pray for your ways and not my own. I am weak and entitled. In moments I feel strongly that my ways for my life and future are the best. Help me to be flexible and open with the steps you have for me. Provide me with the courage to easily give up the plans I am set on and let you work and lead me.

Father, help me to overcome the thought that my personal plans for my future will not bring me full joy and satisfaction, they will fail me if I only do it my way. Your ways are always best, and that is all I want.

If your plans fail, where does the hope of your future lie?

Full Expression

No one has ever seen God. But if we love each other,
God lives in us, and his love is brought to full expression in us.
1 JOHN 4:12 NLT

God, help me to reflect your love and selflessness to everyone I encounter. You have called us to love our neighbors as ourselves, help me to take action in that.

Not everyone knows of you, Lord, and the miraculous things you have done and have yet to do. Let me reflect on you, for that is what I want others to notice. Help me to encourage and uplift the people you have put around me. Bring your love to full expression in me.

Where do you see God's love at work in the lives of those around you?

Still Promised

"For I know the plans I have for you," declares the LORD,
"plans to prosper you and not to harm you,
plans to give you hope and a future."
JEREMIAH 29:11 NIV

Lord, help me to have patience in your plans for me. I feel the need to want everything here and now, and that is not what you have planned. Help me to have an open heart and patience to wait and rely on you.

God, the waiting season is so beautiful and beneficial and should not be rushed. Your plans will always be what I need even though I might think differently. I want to completely trust you and the process. You have good plans for me. I believe it. I place my hope in that promise.

Is your hope in your own plans or in God's goodness?

Jealousy

Wrath is fierce and anger is a flood,
But who can stand before jealousy?
PROVERBS 27:4 NASB

God, I don't want to be robbed by jealousy. It is so easy to want what my friends or family members have. I don't want to fall into entitlement and thinking that I deserve something when you have something better for me.

Help me to have the mindset of being thankful for the circumstances I am in and grateful for the things I have in my life. I don't want to be robbed of anything you have for me. Gratitude is the perfect weapon against jealousy. I want to walk in thanksgiving before you and others because you have given me so much and I truly am thankful.

Has envy kept you from enjoying what you have?

Reconciliation

If while we were enemies we were reconciled to God
by the death of his Son, much more, now that we are reconciled,
shall we be saved by his life.
ROMANS 5:10 ESV

Lord, I thank you for making an impact on my life. I thank you for seeing me as worth fighting for. I am humbly overwhelmed by the gifts you give to me each and every day. I thank you that every morning I wake up and experience a new day and I get to receive your peace and joy. No person will ever be capable of filling me fully with love and affection as you do.

God, thank you for meeting me where I was, a sinner in need of a Savior, and giving me salvation and life. I am amazed by your goodness.

How has your relationship with Jesus changed your life?

Beauty in Pain

"In the same way I will not cause pain
without allowing something new to be born," says the LORD.
"If I cause you the pain, I will not stop you from giving birth
to your new nation," says your God.
ISAIAH 66:9 NCV

God, I don't fully understand why harmful things happen in my life. I sometimes get mad and frustrated because I never go into something and intend on getting hurt. It takes a lot out of me and my heart. You know everything, and you have a plan and purpose for even the most horrible things that take place in my life. I need to understand that you use it all to help grow me and my character.

At the moment I don't fully understand that; help me to lean on you and trust that everything you allow to take place in my life will become something beneficial and beautiful. At the end of birth pains, you bring life and joy. I am expecting that from you in my current situation because I am submitting myself to you in it.

Can you see beauty that came out of painful times in your life?

Already Won

"The LORD your God is the one who goes with you to fight for you against your enemies to give you victory."

DEUTERONOMY 20:4 NIV

Lord, I thank you that every single day you fight for me. I need to learn to take courage and be strong no matter what the circumstance.

God for you are bigger than any giant I face. I don't want fear to overcome my mind because fear is not from you. I have full confidence that you have never had the thought of leaving me. You love me more than I could ever imagine, and I am so grateful to receive that overflowing love from you.

What battles are you tired of fighting on your own?

A Right Motivation

"What does it profit them if they gain the whole world,
but lose or forfeit themselves?"

LUKE 9:25 NRSV

God, I want everything I do to be glorifying to you. I want
what you have for me and not what the world does.
The world leads me in a path of unrighteousness and
selfishness, and I don't want my goals and ambitions to
be filled with that.

I want you to inspire the steps I take with plans that
I make for my future. I know if I base my goals and
mindset in what culture or the world wants me to do, it
will fail. I want my steps to go in the direction you have
for me, Lord.

What motivations are driving your goals?

Defeat Is Impossible

Then you will prosper, if you take care to fulfill the statutes and judgments with which the LORD charged Moses concerning Israel. Be strong and of good courage; do not fear nor be dismayed.

1 CHRONICLES 22:13 NKJV

Lord, I pray you would give me confidence and courage within myself. I am so quick to be down and speak negatively about myself. I need to be reminded that I am fearfully and wonderfully made in your image. I need to believe in myself and the qualifications and gifts you have blessed me with.

Father, I don't want anything to stand in between the words you have spoken over me. I want to arise and have confidence, and I want it to show that I truly believe what you have spoken over me. I will be strong and take my courage in you.

What unknown outcomes are keeping you from showing up with courage?

As I Know It

This world and its desires are in the process of passing away,
but those who love to do the will of God live forever.

1 JOHN 2:17 TPT

God, help me to look forward to the things ahead. It
is so easy for me to get stuck in the "now." There are
circumstances in life that have me stuck and feeling
helpless. Allow me to see what you see.

Lord, you say to take things one day at a time. I don't
want to sit and dwell in the negative, for there is no
beneficial movement in doing that. I will sing your praises
in the pleasant and difficult seasons. You are worthy of it
all. Glorious things are ahead.

When this life has you feeling discouraged, do you take
hope that there is a better life in store?

Wisdom and Might

"With God are wisdom and might;
he has counsel and understanding."
JOB 12:13 ESV

Lord, I ask that you would provide me with your wisdom. I pray that I will take captive what you advise me to. It is easy for me to listen and say I will do something about it. I want to put into action the advice and wisdom you have given me.

God, you have so much wisdom and insight to give, and every word is rich. I can grow and flourish from your every breath. I pray I will take action on what you have spoken to me so I don't miss important opportunities that you are providing me with.

What do you need wisdom for right now?

Pursuing Peace

Pursue peace with everyone, and the holiness
without which no one will see the Lord.
HEBREWS 12:14 NRSV

God, you provide a peace that passes all understanding.
It flows with such sweetness and yet such power. I pray it
will flow through me and I will accept it. I have moments
where I feel so anxious and lose sight of where my focus
should be.

In the moments where I am fearful and anxious, I lose
sight of who I should be going to for peace and structure.
I look to things of this world because they are easy to
access, but they will not be sufficient. Your peace is
always present and so beautiful. I pray I would continue
to come to you in my highest moments of stress because
you present me with perfect peace.

What does pursuing peace look like in your life?

It Will Be Done

I also persevered in the work on this wall, and we acquired no land, and all my servants were gathered there for the work.
NEHEMIAH 5:16 ESV

Lord, I pray you would give me the strength to do everything to the best of my abilities. Things like work and school can be very overwhelming and I tend to lack motivation.

You see everything, God. You know what I struggle with and what I stress about when it comes to putting my time and dedication to something. I pray you would give me the determination to do my best and be proud of my work and effort. I will persevere in doing what I believe you have called me to because I know you will give me the strength I need to get the job done.

Are you feeling the pressure of work that seems never-ending?

Loved to Love

> "This is My commandment,
> that you love one another,
> just as I have loved you."
> JOHN 15:12 NASB

God, I pray that I would treat others how you treat them. You always love and care for others and expect absolutely nothing in return. You are forever selfless and gracious to every single person you have placed on this earth.

As a human, I don't always see the good outcomes of loving every person in my life. I have enemies, and I don't want to show them compassion or grace. You would though, Lord, and I pray I would live out the example you have set for me.

What does it mean to love like Jesus?

Beautiful Reflection

One thing I ask from the LORD, this only do I seek:
that I may dwell in the house of the LORD all the days of my life,
to gaze on the beauty of the LORD and to seek him in his temple.
PSALM 27:4 NIV

God, I am so thankful that I get to experience you every day. I pray that I never get the desire to leave, for nothing is more satisfying than being in your presence. You fill me up and constantly speak truth over me and my life. You don't ever give your heart in pieces; you give it all in one.

Father, you have loved me over and over regardless of how many times I have messed up and sinned. No one has ever loved me the way you have and continue to do. Help me to keep seeking you and your presence every single day, for I am truly satisfied when I do.

How is the life of Jesus reflected in your life?

More than Enough

They will not be disgraced in hard times;
even in famine they will have more than enough.
PSALM 37:19 NLT

Lord, this world honestly hurts. There is pain I experience that breaks me down. I feel weak and unmotivated and sometimes don't know how to heal. Keeping my head up all the time by myself becomes so difficult. I forget in these moments that you want me to come to you. You always have your arms wide open and you are ready for me to run into them.

Father, you want me to deal with whatever healing process is necessary for me to go through but never on my own. You hurt when you see me broken and feeling alone. I thank you that you see me and want all my brokenness. I pray that I always run to you first with my pain and confusion.

Where do you find your security in hard times?

Call Out

"Then you will call upon Me and go and pray to Me,
and I will listen to you."

JEREMIAH 29:12 NKJV

Father God, I pray that you would provide me with your complete patience. I tend to rush things that are most impactful when I don't give it the proper time it needs. Good things come to those who wait. I truly need to trust you in the waiting seasons.

Glorious things take time. You can't rush a flower's growth because it will not grow properly. It takes time and patience and it grows into something so gorgeous. It also takes a large amount of nutrients that need time to absorb. Let this be a reminder to me to be patient and not rush the waiting process. I know the outcome is going to be wonderful in its proper timing.

How does waiting make you feel?

Thankful in Trials

Whenever you face trials of any kind, consider it nothing but joy, because you know that the testing of your faith produces endurance; and let endurance have its full effect, so that you may be mature and complete, lacking in nothing.

JAMES 1:2-4 NRSV

Lord, I want to learn to praise you through the good and bad circumstances I face. You are worthy of all my praise. I know that everything I come in contact with is building my character and helps fill my purpose and calling in life.

Father, I will take joy in the moments of trial and I will choose to see the nourishment that difficult times bring rather than only focusing on the negative. I know that you will be with me through every encounter I face, and I thank you for that gift.

What can you be thankful for in the trial you are facing?

Where You Are

"Where two or three are gathered in my name,
there am I among them."
MATTHEW 18:20 ESV

God, I want to surround myself with people who
encourage me in the ways and directions you want me to
go in. I pray that I would have the wisdom and insight to
see the toxic influences in my life and choose to surround
myself with people who speak life. I know you have
placed these impactful people in my life, and I pray that I
would see them and let them speak into my choices and
decisions.

Lord, I need to be with people who purely want the
intentions of bringing glory and praise to your name, for
that is what you put us on this earth for. Please help me to
stick close with the people you highlight as being those
who encourage me in my faith.

Who encourages you in your faith?

May

Your word is like a lamp for my feet
and a light for my path.

PSALM 119:105 NCV

A Glimpse

Certainly there is a future,
And your hope will not be cut off.
PROVERBS 23:18 NASB

Lord, I don't know what you have in store for me. I don't know what is to come; I can only do the best I can day by day. I am extremely grateful that I have you by my side making sure I don't fall. I am human and I make a lot of mistakes, but I thank you that you cover them all.

God, I thank you that your grace is sufficient through the darkest points of my life. I never want to lose hope in you and the plan you have before me. Thank you for always watching out for me and always wanting the best for me.

What hope do you have for the future?

Captives Set Free

We have freedom now, because Christ made us free. So stand strong. Do not change and go back into the slavery of the law.

GALATIANS 5:1 NCV

God, you have blessed me with the choice of free will. I pray that I will make the right choices and decisions. I want to have your discernment over every action I take. Allow me to be cautious of the rules I chose to abide by and take action in.

There are many laws created by this culture, Father. I pray that I would always make choices based on what your Word says and ask you what I should do before I take action.

Are you living bound to the law, or are you living in the freedom that Christ offers?

Not So Different

> "The foreigner residing among you must be treated as your native-born. Love them as yourself, for you were foreigners in Egypt. I am the LORD your God."
>
> LEVITICUS 19:34 NIV

Lord, you have instructed us to love one another. It can be really challenging to love others especially when they have done wrong by me or have projected themselves to be dishonoring and disrespectful people. It can also be a challenge to love others who are different than me.

I pray that I would have no restrictions or fears from loving others. I pray that I would live out your example of love. I was put on this earth to show your love and kindness to everyone I encounter. Help me have the selflessness to put it into action.

Is fear keeping you from loving others who are different than you?

Enemies Will See

"Blessed are those who are persecuted for righteousness' sake,
for theirs is the kingdom of heaven."
MATTHEW 5:10 NKJV

God, I know life as a Christian comes with overwhelming and scary challenges. I pray that I would have the courage and boldness to conquer the challenges and judgment that I face. I know I will meet people who do not agree with the choice I have made to follow you.

The world is filled with harsh criticism, but you are bigger than it all. I pray for fearlessness and the willingness to sacrifice myself for your name. I want to be used by you and bring full glory to you. Give me the courageous heart and passion to accomplish that.

Have you suffered for the sake of the Gospel?

Within the Walls

"Peace be within your walls,
and security within your towers."

PSALM 122:7 NRSV

God, I pray I would not hold onto things so tightly. Sometimes I tend not to let go and allow you to comfort me in difficult times. I know if I fully give you what is holding me back from finding healing I would find peace.

I try to heal by myself but that is not what you want me to be doing. You never see what I am stressing or hurting about as a burden. You love me, broken and all. I am forever grateful to have a God who loves me and is passionate about protecting me. Thank you for the peace I have within the walls of your arms.

When is the last time you felt peace in the middle of chaos?

Inside Out

"Don't judge by his appearance or height, for I have rejected him.
The LORD doesn't see things the way you see them. People judge
by outward appearance, but the LORD looks at the heart."

1 SAMUEL 16:7 NLT

Lord, you have made each individual so uniquely
beautiful and different. Not one person is like the other,
and you see it all as good. You have made us with
different body types and sizes. You have made some with
blue eyes and some with brown. Some you have made
so extremely tall, and others short.

Father, you see every human as beautiful and filled with
purpose. I pray that I would always see people through
your eyes. We all are created for a glorious purpose, and
that is incredible. Help me not to judge others on their
outward appearance but on the actions of their hearts.

How do you judge a person's worth?

When in Doubt

Keep being compassionate to those who still have doubts.
JUDE 1:22 TPT

God, I thank you for all the wonders you have created.
Some I understand and others I have yet to fully
grab a hold of. I sometimes don't understand certain
circumstances that I encounter. That can stir up questions
or concerns. I am thankful that you are open to questions
and don't shut them down.

There are many manipulations from the world and I
only want to know what you and your Word say about
discerning my thoughts and questions. I want your clarity
over my mind when I have difficult questions to ask.

Do you believe that it's okay to have doubts or questions?

Fear No Evil

Even though I walk through the valley of the shadow of death,
I fear no evil, for You are with me;
Your rod and Your staff, they comfort me.
PSALM 23:4 NASB

Lord, the darkness can be so deceiving. I have moments where I feel like the only way to get away from my anxious thoughts and fears is to run and hide. It is so easy to hide in the dark, but I know that is not where I am supposed to be.

Father, it is scary to bring light to my difficult situations, but I know that in the light I find you and my healing. Fears, anxiety, and depression are not from you. I pray that I will find healing in you. Instead of hiding in the darkness I want to bring it to you fully open to your never-ending love and affection. Thank you for loving me in my weak seasons.

How does God's presence affect your level of fear and anxiety?

My Inspiration

All Scripture is given by inspiration of God, and is profitable
for doctrine, for reproof, for correction, for instruction in
righteousness.

2 Timothy 3:16 NKJV

God, I thank you that everything in the Bible is true. It
is incredible to have full access to a book filled with
testimonies and verses that bring light and truth into
every situation. It can be interpreted in so many ways and
is always filled with surprises.

I thank you that it speaks wisdom and also challenges me
in ways that I need to be challenged. I am thankful that
your words have been written and I can take what you
said and use it in everyday situations. It is a true gift to
have the Bible.

How does God's Word inspire you?

All I Am

"Love the LORD your God with all your heart,
all your soul, and all your strength."
DEUTERONOMY 6:5 NCV

God, I want to hold nothing back from you. I want you to have my thoughts, my intentions, my struggles, my passions, and my life. You have given me life on this earth, and it truly isn't mine to have. All of me is yours.

I get so easily wrapped up in my own selfish intentions and desires and I forget that this life I'm living isn't about me. I am put here for the purpose of bringing glory to your name. I don't want to live my life out selfishly. I want to live it for you. I give you permission to work through me and take captive everything I possess. I surrender it all to you.

Is there any part of you that you've been holding back from God?

You Get Me

We do not have a high priest who is unable to empathize with our weaknesses, but we have one who has been tempted in every way, just as we are—yet he did not sin.

HEBREWS 4:15 NIV

Lord, I thank you that you sent your beloved Son down to earth. Jesus was the living example of a perfect human. He had all the temptations and struggles that we face every day here on earth, yet he never sinned. I want to take that example and live it out.

Jesus, you showed me that even though the strongest forces of evil and temptations will come at me, I have the ability and choice to be strong and stand up to it. You lived that out every single day on this earth, and I want to live like you did. It is difficult, but with you anything is possible.

What does it mean to you that God is familiar with your suffering?

Whole Again

The LORD is close to the brokenhearted;
he rescues those whose spirits are crushed.
PSALM 34:17 NLT

God, I have many areas in my life that need your restoration. My heart has been broken in multiple ways by people I am close to. I have put my trust and effort in people and have been let down. I pray for your love to overwhelm me and also give me the heart to forgive. I am a broken vessel without you, and I need you to reassure me that everything is going to be okay.

You see the unseen, and you know every piece of my heart. You see the things that have destroyed and burned me the most even when I won't admit it to myself. I know that you have the right tools and wisdom to nurture me back to health. I am grateful to have you as my rescuer and friend.

What broken parts of your life need the Lord's restoration?

Empathy

Rejoice with those who rejoice,
weep with those who weep.
ROMANS 12:15 NRSV

God, I want to receive the capacity to love people when they are in a rough spot and not be drained. I pray that I would not take people's struggles and put them on myself to fix them. You are the God of mercy and strength, and I pray I would receive that. I pray that over myself, so I can be there fully for other people.

What people close to me face isn't a burden; you have placed me in their life to be a guide back to you. You do not run from harmful situations. You are forever consistent. I pray for a heart capacity like yours.

What does it cost you to relate to others without trying to fix them?

As It Should Be

If we know he hears us every time we ask him,
we know we have what we ask from him.

1 JOHN 5:15 NCV

Lord, I pray that I would trust you to provide for me when the time is right. I tend to live selfishly and get frustrated when things don't go my way. Where does that truly get me? I pray that I would sacrifice and give up my desires and trust your timing. In all honesty, it is a struggle to give things up. I am human and most often entitled which is not how I am supposed to act. What example does that set for other people?

Father, I want to sacrifice my desires and give them fully to you, for you know my purpose. I am also thankful that you do know the desires of my heart, and you don't ignore my passions. I want to follow what you have for me, for I trust it will be beautiful in its time.

Do you believe that God provides all that you need?

Living on Camera

Whoever walks in integrity walks securely,
but he who makes his ways crooked will be found out.
PROVERBS 10:9 ESV

God, it is very easy for me to get hyped up on all the things that the world provides. I get caught up in people and events and I allow that to be my source of joy and happiness. In moments, I find myself valuing the excitement I get from being around people who are toxic or events that make me lose my character. I live for myself, and that is not what I was put on this earth for.

Lord, you give me people and items to enjoy, but that should not be my only source of joy. I want my joy and passion to come from you because I know you will never fail me. You will never let me down like the things of this world do. God, help me to be accountable.

Are you living to please God or yourself?

Glorified

I know that I have not yet reached that goal,
but there is one thing I always do.
Forgetting the past and straining toward what is ahead.
PHILIPPIANS 3:13 NCV

Lord, I pray that I would never look back. I want to focus on you and what you have yet to bring into my life. I know that you let circumstances come into my life to learn and grow from them. I pray that my mind and heart would not dwell on those situations. You have great and beneficial things in store for me.

God, focusing on what I have done in the past will hold me back from getting eager and ready for what you have. I don't want to be set back from focusing on distractions, for I know that is what the enemy wants me to do. I pray I would look forward to you.

What has been keeping you from moving forward in faith?

Father of Goodness

Praise the LORD in song, for He has done glorious things;
Let this be known throughout the earth.

ISAIAH 12:5 NASB

I thank you, Lord, for all the wondrous beauty you have placed in my life. I apologize that I don't take time to enjoy it or give you glory for it. You never cease to blow me away. I tend to focus on all the negative in my life, and I pray I wouldn't gravitate toward that. When I do that, I miss out on so much that you are eager and excited for me to experience.

God, I want to take the time to thank you and appreciate all that you have created, and also to thank you for all the incredible influences you have placed in my life. I take and receive all the glorious wonders you have blessed me with.

Where do you see the goodness of God in your life?

Life Gets Busy

The Lord answered her, "Martha, my beloved Martha. Why are you upset and troubled, pulled away by all these many distractions? Are they really that important? Mary has discovered the one thing most important by choosing to sit at my feet. She is undistracted, and I won't take this privilege from her."

LUKE 10:41-42 TPT

God, I want to experience you in the quietness. I do believe that you are most present in those moments. I get caught up in all the chaos and busyness that life provides. I pray that I would make an effort to take time out of my day and sacrifice it to you to just sit in silence in your presence. Your presence is so beautiful and impactful. I can obtain so much by simply tuning out all distractions and listening to what you have to say.

Father, in this day and age it is so hard to remove myself from distractions. I need to be reminded that every moment spent with you is worth it. There has never been a moment in time where being with you was destructive. So, show me what I need to set aside in order to spend time with you.

How can you practice sitting in the presence of God in the middle of a busy day or season?

With You

We can confidently say,
"The LORD is my helper;
I will not fear;
what can man do to me?"
HEBREWS 13:6 ESV

Lord, I pray that I would not be overwhelmed by the difficult circumstances that I face. I know that you are bigger than anything I come in contact with. I lose sight of how mighty a God you are. There is nothing in this world that makes you stumble or fear.

You are the Lord of lords, and King of kings and nothing can stand against you. I pray that I would never lose sight of that and always come to you no matter what I face. You are my helper. No one can do anything to me when you are standing beside me.

What do you need God's help with today?

In the Fight

The godly may trip seven times, but they will get up again. But one disaster is enough to overthrow the wicked.

PROVERBS 24:16 NLT

God, I thank you for all the strength you have given me. Help me use that strength to listen to your Word. I pray that you would teach me how to continuously try again. With you I know that I am not weak-minded. You hold me in your hands and you know everything about me, so I know that I am not alone.

Father, you have given me the power I need to start over. Teach me the best ways to be devoted to trying again. Help me desire to keep going even when I want to give up. Show me how to guard my heart from lies and the sins of the world, so I don't get caught up in disaster. I pray that I will be faithful and devoted to you even when I fall.

What keeps you getting up when you fall?

CFW

Absent of Judgment

"Do not judge, and you will not be judged;
do not condemn, and you will not be condemned.
Forgive, and you will be forgiven."

LUKE 6:37 NRSV

Lord, I thank you for all you teach me. I know that sometimes I fail, but you provide me with grace. I pray that I will not be quick to judge but I will learn how to help others through their challenges as you do for me.

There are times when it is hard for me to forgive. I pray that you would teach me how to easily forgive others even when they have hurt me or have made me upset. Sometimes I wonder if I could ever forgive someone for something they did, but with your unconditional love, I know that I can.

Are you quick to judge those who offend you?

CFW

Honoring Family

Whoever does not care for his own relatives, especially his own family members, has turned against the faith and is worse than someone who does not believe in God.

1 TIMOTHY 5:8 NCV

There are times when it is hard for me to care about what my family thinks or feels, but I want to be better about that, Jesus. I pray that you would help me to grow a deeper connection with my family. I want that connection to be strong like your love for me. Help me grow deeper in love with my family and the time we share together.

I pray that the connection would be Spirit-filled and that we can all grow in your love together. I know that sometimes I might want to follow my own ideas or I believe that I can do things on my own but help me honor my family by keeping them close because I need them, Jesus.

How do you honor the Lord with your family?

CFW

No Striving

"My presence will go with you,
and I will give you rest."
EXODUS 33:14 ESV

God, with you I feel peace. Even when I am lonely, I am never fully alone. You are right beside me and you love me unconditionally. There have been times when I forget that you are there for me, but when you show me that you are, it's when I needed a reminder the most.

When I sit and spend time with you, I feel the peace that you bring me. I feel joy. Sometimes I stray from your presence and I forget that feeling. But even during those times you are there and you love me just the same. Help me to devote myself to you during the good and bad times. I need your presence to give me rest.

What can you stop working so hard at on your own?

Lesser Things

Let what you heard from the beginning abide in you.
If what you heard from the beginning abides in you,
then you will abide in the Son and in the Father.
1 JOHN 2:24 NRSV

Father, there are things in this world that try to take me away from what I know. Help me to stick to my gut feeling. When I feel that something is wrong, it's often because of you. You tell me what I need to know and what I should do. There are values that I have in my life and know are important, and I ask for your guidance to stick to those values even when I don't want to.

God, when I go against what I know and believe, I feel guilt in my stomach and a churning in my heart. I ask for your forgiveness when I give in to sin. There are times when I am confused, but I pray you would tell me what I need to do and help guide me through it.

What kingdom values are evident in your life?

CFW

Better than Winning

When you do things, do not let selfishness or pride be your guide.
Instead, be humble and give more honor to others
than to yourselves.

PHILIPPIANS 2:3 NCV

Why is it easier to do something for yourself than it is
for others? Jesus, help me desire to show love toward
everyone. I want to be more like you. Sometimes I do
things for myself without considering how it could affect
someone else. And other times I try to hide that I care for
people because I don't want to hurt myself, but people
need to know that they are loved. I know that doing
things for others may take more time and consideration,
but it is worth it in the end because I know that I will be
more like you.

Lord, I pray that you would give me the strength to share
your love with everyone around me. I want people to
know that they are loved unconditionally, just like I am.

Is honoring someone else over your own agenda worth
it to you?

CFW

Increase My Faith

The apostles said to the Lord,
"Increase our faith."
LUKE 17:5 NLT

God, I see you in the little things: the sunsets, the warm
weather, the stars, and the birds chirping in the morning.
But sometimes I lose sight of my faith for you. When I get
caught up in my own little world and my own selfishness,
I forget what you have taught me. When my faith wavers
you are still there waiting patiently.

Keep my faith strong and my heart for you even stronger.
I surrender my life to you, Jesus. You died on a cross for
someone like me. Why is that so hard to remember? The
compassion and grace you have for me is unmatchable.
Help me stay faithful to you even during my worst
moments because you do the same for me.

What do you need more faith for?

CFW

Unmerited Favor

Remember this: sin will not conquer you, for God already has!
You are not governed by law but governed by the reign
of the grace of God.

ROMANS 6:14 TPT

God, I forget how strong you are. Sometimes it feels
like sin controls me, but you are stronger than any sin. I
am so thankful for the grace you have given me. I have
made mistakes and I regret them, but when I ask for your
forgiveness, it is already done. I have often thought that
I could not be forgiven but then I remember your grace
and devotion.

Father, you judge fairly and know what intentions have
been in my heart and what thoughts are in my mind. You
know what I want and what I need. I ask you to remind
me that you are stronger than anything I am going
through and any temptation of my mind.

What has the most power over your thought life?

CFW

Not Hidden

All my longings lie open before you, LORD;
my sighing is not hidden from you.
PSALM 38:9 NIV

Jesus, you know everything about me. You know more than anyone will ever understand and you know me more than I know myself. Everything I have is in your hands. I pray that you will guide me through the challenges that will come. I cannot hide from you. Sometimes I forget that even though you know the worst things about me, you give me grace.

God, I pray that you would help me to continuously be open with you. When I am most hurt, I am reminded of who I can run to, but help me to remember that even when I am happy. Help me to understand that you are the only person that can fully heal my heart.

Is there anything you've been trying to hide from the Lord?

CFW

Goodness Shared

Do not forget to do good and to share,
for with such sacrifices God is well pleased.
HEBREWS 13:16 NKJV

Jesus, please remind me what I can do to show others that I love them. Make these actions be out of love and not selfishness. I want to be like you. Sometimes I want to do my own thing and feel a certain way but help me to change my attitude and be willing to do something for someone else.

God, please provide me with examples of how I can best show your love for others. I want to please you and show how much I love you. I know that sometimes the best way of doing that is by sacrificing something of my own for another person.

How do you share the goodness of your life with others?

CFW

Unconditional Acceptance

"Everything that the Father gives Me will come to Me,
and the one who comes to Me I will certainly not cast out."

JOHN 6:37 NASB

Father, at times it's hard for me to remember that you accept me through everything. I know there are times when it is hard for me to follow your ways, but you still accept me. I pray that you would help me do this for others as well. It is difficult to always love people and accept them in spite of the things they do, but I know that you would want me to do that.

Jesus, please help me learn what I should surround myself with. Help me grow stronger in my faith so I am prepared to help those who need you the most. Teach me not to judge others but to accept them and bring them into faith in you.

Do you believe that every part of you is fully accepted by God?

Aim for Harmony

Let us aim for harmony in the church
and try to build each other up.

ROMANS 14:19 NLT

Lord, help me to surround myself with those who follow you. When I am with people who know you, there is a deeper connection between us. I pray that you would help me learn the best way to keep harmony in the church. Teach me to be an example for those in my church and help me to be a peacekeeper.

God, instead of tearing others down, I want to show your love and remind them of what it is like to be with you. I want my church to be a place where people feel your unconditional love right as they enter the doors.

Is harmony or order more important in a church setting?

CFW

June

I pray that the God who gives hope
will fill you with much joy and peace
while you trust in him. Then your
hope will overflow by the power
of the Holy Spirit.

ROMANS 15:13 NCV

Dependable

Let not steadfast love and faithfulness forsake you;
bind them around your neck;
write them on the tablet of your heart.
PROVERBS 3:3 ESV

God, love is hard. There are many different ways to show love, but sometimes it is hard for me to be vulnerable. It is important to guard my heart and mind, but it is also important to love others. I pray for your guidance to understand the difference.

Father, protect me from those who might hurt me, but help me show them that they can depend on me if they need me. I am strong, but with you I am strongest. People may turn on me and be unkind but I know that your love will not forsake me.

Would your friends and family describe you as being dependable?

I Will Rejoice

This is the day the LORD has made;
We will rejoice and be glad in it.
PSALM 118:24 NKJV

Father, thank you for all that you do. Every day you are with me and you walk with me. I want to thank you for each day you have given me on this earth. I am excited to be in your kingdom and rejoice with you. You have given me so much and I am so thankful for that.

Lord, each day you bless me even if I don't know it. I appreciate even the bad days that I have gone through because many of them I have learned a lesson. Jesus, please help me to be reminded that each day I am on earth is a blessing and that you are the one guiding me through it.

What can you rejoice in today?

CFW

With All

"Love the LORD your God with all your heart,
all your soul, all your strength, and all your mind."
Also, "Love your neighbor as you love yourself."
LUKE 10:27 NCV

Jesus, sometimes I have a hard time telling others about you. I worry that someone is going to judge me or look at me differently. But even if they do, I could change their life and bring them into the faith which is so much better than knowing I didn't say anything.

Father, I pray that you would help me become better at this. I want my friends to be in your kingdom with me. Remind me that loving others is just as important as loving myself. Help me to focus on relationships in my life and devote myself to showing your love to those who need it. It's harder to love someone that treats me unkindly, but I know that through you I can do anything.

Are any parts of you holding back from loving God?

CFW

Every Moment

Teach us to number our days,
that we may gain a heart of wisdom.

PSALM 90:12 NIV

God, not every choice I have made was for you. I ask for your grace and I pray that you would help me to continuously choose you. I forget that there are limited days on earth and that all of those days I should be praising your name and thanking you for all you have done.

Father, help me to be wise and make good decisions that reflect your love to those around me. I want my values to be an example of you and my heart to be for you only. I know that the best way for me to gain wisdom is by spending time with you, so help me to become better at this.

Are you living with eternity's values in view?

Everything Right

After you suffer for a short time, God, who gives all grace, will
make everything right. He will make you strong and support you
and keep you from falling. He called you to share in his glory in
Christ, a glory that will continue forever.

1 PETER 5:10 NCV

God, when I need someone to go to, you are always
there for me. There have been times when I am hurt, but
I know that I can run to you and you will love and accept
me. I pray that when I am hurting most I won't forget that
you are here for me. With your strength I know that if I fall
I can get up again.

Father, with you I am stronger, and I can get through
anything. I'm amazed by the grace you give me and how
you never let me down when I need you. Help me to
remind others that you are there for them as well and you
won't ever fail them.

Where do you need God's grace to keep you
from falling?

Humble Help

> If another believer is overcome by some sin, you who are godly
> should gently and humbly help that person back onto the right
> path. And be careful not to fall into the same temptation yourself.
> GALATIANS 6:1 NLT

Jesus, I thank you that you are always willing to help me through the hardest times in my life. I pray that you would help me remind those around me of your grace. It is hard to not fall into the same temptations of the people who are closest to me, but you are stronger than all of my temptations and sin.

God, sometimes people do not want to change their ways, but I pray that you would help me guide them back to faith and help me do it gently. Help me show them that I only want to support them and not judge them for whatever sins they have committed.

How do you approach those who are living under the weight of sin?

CFW

Faithful to Forgive

*If we confess our sins, he who is faithful and just
will forgive us our sins and cleanse us from all unrighteousness.*
1 JOHN 1:9 NRSV

Lord, help me to remember that you are gracious and will forgive me for all of my sins. I pray that you will show me how to ask for your forgiveness, but most of all help me to be thankful for your forgiveness and not ashamed to ask for it. Every so often, I forget that you wash away my sins entirely, and I think that I am not cleansed. You see all sins the same way; one isn't greater than the other. And you still forgive me.

God, teach me to do the same for others. I don't want to hold grudges or be easily angered. Remind me of what it is like to continuously forgive and love people.

Are you willing to forgive those who have wronged you?

CFW

We Are Family

I bow my knees before the Father, from whom
every family in heaven and on earth is named.
EPHESIANS 3:14-15 ESV

Father, there is something about being connected
through the Holy Spirit that is so life changing. Having
people surround me that know you and want to be closer
to you makes me so thankful for them in my life. When I
am with those people it is easy to feel like family and to
choose you.

I pray that I would be a light for people who don't know
you and that I would want them to become a part of this
family. Help me to stay strong around these people and
to show you not only through my words but my actions
as well. I want to show everyone that you are what they
need and you will never fail them. Most of all, I want them
to feel welcome in your kingdom.

Do you treat others with the same respect or
compassion that you would a family member?

CFW

My Deepest Pain

"Blessed are those who mourn,
for they will be comforted."
MATTHEW 5:4 NASB

God, when I am hurt so deeply and I feel your presence, I feel peace. I am so comforted when you are around and that is because I know that you love and accept me. I ask that I would not forget that feeling, and that even when I am not mourning, I would still choose your presence.

Father, I have been hurt by people I love and sometimes it is so hard to move past what happened, but I ask that you would help me to forgive them. Occasionally I think about how I should seek your presence, but then I choose something over you. I am sorry. Help me to be stronger and to always choose you as my source of comfort.

In your deepest pain, have you known the comfort of God's presence?

CFW

Pay It Forward

You must show mercy to others, or God will not show mercy to you when he judges you. But the person who shows mercy can stand without fear at the judgment.

JAMES 2:13 NCV

Father God, when I am weak, it is hard for me to forgive and easy to judge. But I ask you to give me strength to show mercy and grace to others. Sometimes if I am angry, my emotions can get out of hand and I say something I don't mean or I do something that I know is wrong. I ask for your forgiveness and your guidance through these times.

God, why is it harder to be a delight to those who you love? I ask that you would teach me how to always be kind and forgiving even when I don't want to. I do not want to fear you when my day of judgment comes. I want to be completely open and dedicated to you.

When dealing with difficult people, are you quick to judge them?

CFW

Security

"I will heal them and reveal
to them abundance of prosperity and security."
JEREMIAH 33:6 ESV

God, thank you for all you do for me. There isn't a day that goes by that you aren't watching over me. I might turn away from you, but you will never do the same to me. I know that you keep me safe and you bring me success. You are the reason I am alive and in you I am more alive than ever before.

Jesus, when I indulge in your presence, I feel comforted and I know that I can trust you with my life. I ask that you would remind me of these feelings so that you are the first thing I run to. Not only do you keep me safe and heal me, but you also heal my heart from sin and evil. Thank you!

Where do you feel safest in your life?

Seek First

"Seek first His kingdom and His righteousness,
and all these things will be provided to you."
MATTHEW 6:33 NASB

Lord, I ask that you would keep me away from selfish acts so I am reminded to choose you over other things. Whenever I have chosen sin over you, I have felt guilty. I ask for your wisdom and strength to keep me away from these sins. Keep me motivated to change things in my life that tempt me to sin.

God, when I want something, if I ask you first, I receive it because you are good or I learn how to accept that I don't need it because I trust you. There isn't a time when you haven't been faithful to me. So why is it hard for me to stay faithful to you? Help me to surrender myself to you every day.

What are the motivations of the plans you make?

CFW

Reason for Success

The LORD will be your confidence,
And will keep your foot from being caught.
PROVERBS 3:26 NASB

Jesus, sometimes I am ashamed of myself. It is hard for me to love who I am or what I have done. I know that I have sinned, but sometimes I forget that's not the only thing you look at. I have been looking for love and when I feel it, I start to feel more confident in myself, but I've been looking in the wrong place. You are what I should have been looking for.

Father, I get distracted and caught up in myself, but I can look to you and find unconditional love that can't be replaced. I forget how to be confident when I think about my mistakes or flaws, but you can build me up. I pray that I wouldn't forget that when I stop believing in myself.

Do you have more confidence in your abilities or in God's?

CFW

Rightly Placed Trust

When I am afraid,
I will put my trust in you.
PSALM 56:3 NLT

Jesus, I don't want to be afraid anymore. When I know you are with me, I feel peace and I am stronger. I can't replace that feeling with anything. I have a hard time trusting especially when I have been forsaken. But you won't forsake me and you never have. You are faithful and trustworthy. I pray that your trust is all I need.

God, I have looked for trust in other relationships and each one hasn't been the same as the relationship I have with you. When fear overtakes my life, I feel weak. I know that you protect me from this fear. I pray that I wouldn't forget that and that I would run to you both when I am weak and when I am strong.

What do you do with fear when it overtakes you?

CFW

Bloom

Grow in the grace and knowledge
of our Lord and Savior Jesus Christ.
To him be glory both now and forever! Amen.

2 PETER 3:18 NIV

God, I ask that I would devote my time to you. Walking out my faith is a daily surrender. I need to spend time with you to grow closer to, and stronger in, you. I want to be able to praise your name whenever and wherever I am. Even though sometimes this is hard for me to do, I want to do it.

Father, you have always been gracious and strong. I pray that you would help me to do the same. If I am like you, I can make others feel loved and I can welcome them into your presence. But I cannot do this when I don't spend time with you and don't know you. I pray that I would want to grow closer to you.

Do you see the fruit of God's kingdom at work in your life as you grow in him?

Thoughts Captured

Think about the things that are good and worthy of praise.
Think about the things that are true and honorable and right
and pure and beautiful and respected.

PHILIPPIANS 4:8 NCV

There are so many things in this world that I can see you in. Jesus, sometimes my thoughts go places that they shouldn't. I think constantly. I overthink a lot of situations from the past which brings me anxiety and stress. I pray that you would help me to overcome this and leave it in your hands.

Father, I know that if I give these things to you, I can trust that you will do what is best for me even if it isn't the choice I want. I pray that you would keep me sturdy in my faith even when unclean thoughts cloud my mind and judgment.

Do you pay attention to where your thoughts go throughout the day?

Choose Your Way

A man without self-control
is like a city broken into and left without walls.
PROVERBS 25:28 ESV

God, I have known what self-control feels like, but sometimes it is hard to do this when there are so many temptations. When I don't have control, I can feel how unstable everything is. I feel weak and weary. If I follow what I know is right and I don't fall into temptation, I feel how much sturdier my life is. This is because I am following you and what you have taught me.

Jesus, even though I don't always follow what I know is good for my soul, you give me grace and I learn from what I did wrong. Thank you for guiding me.

Do you actively put up healthy boundaries in your life?

Good Sense

Those with good sense are slow to anger,
and it is their glory to overlook an offense.
PROVERBS 19:11 NRSV

Father, when I am weak, it is easier for me to quickly get angry. Sometimes my chest burns with anger. But when I tell myself that you will take care of it, that burning sensation leaves my body completely. It is easiest to feel angered when someone I really care for does something to me or to others that I think is wrong. I pray that you would change how I feel about this.

God, help me to easily love others and just as easily forgive them. When someone offends me, I want to be able to forget what they said and remember that whatever they have to say can never change what you think of me and how you love me.

Are you quick to anger?

Contentment

Each of you should continue to live in whatever situation the Lord
has placed you, and remain as you were when God first called you.
1 CORINTHIANS 7:17 NLT

Lord, help me to know the difference between what
situation you have put me in and what situation
I shouldn't be in. When I feel like I don't belong
somewhere, my first instinct is to want to leave. Help me
to be content in the place I am in even if I don't want to
be there. You do things for a reason, and you will put me
where you need me to show your love.

Father, I pray that I will grow closer to you so I feel what
you want me to do and so I don't get caught up in other
things in this world. I know there are ways that I can show
your faithfulness to others where I am right now but show
me where you want me most.

Where does your contentment come from?

CFW

Ultimate Guide

I want you to pattern your lives after me,
just as I pattern mine after Christ.
1 CORINTHIANS 11:1 TPT

God, remind me to follow you before others. I know that you are what I need most, and it is important for me to spend time with you. Jesus, you are my strongest guide. If I follow you, I know that I will not be forsaken. Show me what I can do to follow your footsteps.

Father, if I am going to be a part of your kingdom, I want to bring others with me. I want people to know what it is like to have you in their life. Sometimes I forget how lucky I am to have you with me. Help me to follow your guide and to not stray far from your Word.

What leads you in life?

CFW

Nothing to Condemn

There is now no condemnation at all
for those who are in Christ Jesus.

ROMANS 8:1 NASB

Jesus, when I fail, I don't always remember the grace you have for me. I know that I make mistakes, but I don't always know that you are still there for me. When I repent of my sins, I feel the weight leave my shoulders and I have relief. I receive that feeling because of your forgiveness.

Father, it is hard for me to forgive others, but sometimes it is harder for me to forgive myself. Even if I forgive myself, I often look back at sins I have committed and I feel guilty again. Why am I hard on myself even when I know I am forgiven? Please teach me the best way to move past the mistakes I have made and repented of. I know there is no condemnation in you.

When you make mistakes, do you feel the weight of condemnation or the relief of God's covering grace?

CFW

Small Faith

"You don't have enough faith," Jesus told them. "I tell you the truth, if you had faith even as small as a mustard seed, you could say to this mountain, 'Move from here to there,' and it would move. Nothing would be impossible."

MATTHEW 17:20 NLT

Lord, I want my faith to grow stronger. Why is it so easy to forget faith? I have to continuously be devoting myself to you. It's true that with you nothing is impossible, but for some reason I still question things. I know that I am not alone in this; others question you as well. I pray that you would help me and other followers to stay strong and remember your grace and all that you have done.

Father, I wish that I didn't question you, but sometimes my questioning keeps my faith strong because I look at all you have done in my life and I know that you have always been there for me. I am so thankful.

What impossible situation is waiting for you to step out in faith?

Selflessness

Let each of you look out not only for his own interests,
but also for the interests of others.
PHILIPPIANS 2:4 NKJV

Jesus, when I help others, it makes me feel closer to you.
You are so kind and you always do things for people. I
ask that you would remind me to do this. I don't want to
be selfish. If I give up my time and show acts of love, I
know that you would be grateful. I want to please you.

Help me to indulge in acts of service and compassion
for others. I know that it is important to watch my own
actions and what things I am participating in or what I put
my heart toward, but it's equally as important to notice
others and care for them.

How can you practice selflessness today?

No Shame

> Do your best to present yourself to God as one approved by him,
> a worker who has no need to be ashamed, rightly explaining
> the word of truth.
> 2 Timothy 2:15 NRSV

Father, when I sin, I want to be able to run to your arms, but sometimes I am ashamed of myself. I ask myself why I decided to do something wrong even when I knew what the right thing to do was. I need to be reminded that even though I feel this way, I can still go to you with an open heart. As I come to you, I want to be confident and tell you the whole truth.

God, you already know my heart and my mind, so being open with you is easier and I am grateful for that. You don't need me to tell you the sins I have committed because you already know them, but you want me to tell you and repent because when I do, I am opening my heart up to you.

What in others makes you proud to know them?

Take Courage

"Have I not commanded you?
Be strong and of good courage;
do not be afraid, nor be dismayed,
for the LORD your God is with you wherever you go."
JOSHUA 1:9 NKJV

Jesus, I know that I can trust your Word. Even when I am not strong in my faith, you are with me. Even when I doubt you, you are with me. Even when I am discouraged and I feel alone, you are with me!

God, I know that you are always going to be here for me and I thank you for that. I pray that I would try to do the same for you. I want to spend more time with you. You give me the courage and strength I need to get through the day. My life feels worthless without you. I wouldn't have the durability I need to try again if I didn't have you in my life.

What do you need courage to face today?

CFW

Forgive Me

Consider my affliction and my trouble,
and forgive all my sins.
PSALM 25:18 ESV

God, there is never a time you don't forgive me for my sin. I want to fully believe that. I have doubted that you forgive me completely and I have been ashamed of myself. Your grace is so great. Every time I fall down, you are there to pick me up. You are so dependable and that is hard to find nowadays.

Jesus, I have been troubled and confused but when I needed you the most you were there for me. I don't need anyone else. I keep searching for things when all I need is to see that you are right here and you are all that I need.

Do you believe that when you ask for it, you receive full forgiveness?

CFW

Living Water

"He who believes in Me, as the Scripture has said,
out of his heart will flow rivers of living water."

JOHN 7:38 NKJV

God, when I surrendered my life to you, I didn't know how my life would change. But you are constant and I don't need to worry. When I spend time with you, I feel more alive than ever before. There's a burning passion in my heart for you. I ask that you keep that fire strong. I praise your name and I am alive! I pray that my heart would be only for you. You are all I need.

Lord, I want to share that passion in my heart with believers that are struggling and those who have not come to know you yet. Help me show your love to people who don't believe in you. People who are alone don't know that they could have you with them. I don't understand how, but you love everyone equally, and I ask that you would help me do the same.

What is flowing from your heart lately?

CFW

Returned Forgiveness

*"If you forgive those who sin against you,
your heavenly Father will forgive you.
But if you refuse to forgive others,
your Father will not forgive your sins."*

MATTHEW 6:14-15 NLT

There is so much I have learned from you, Father. I might struggle with forgiveness, but I know that it is easier if I am faithful to you. If I have your love in my heart, I am not alone and I know that. Remind me to forgive people even when I don't want to. I don't want hate to be in my heart. I don't want to feel trapped by sin or evils that were sent to destroy me.

Jesus, if I have you in my heart I know that I can give grace like you do. I want my sins to be forgiven by you, but I don't want that to be the only reason I am forgiving others. If I were to do that, it would be selfish. Teach me to forgive easily without wanting anything in return.

Who do you need grace to forgive?

CFW

Fully Known

"The very hairs of your head are all numbered."
MATTHEW 10:30 NKJV

Jesus, I am so amazed by you. You know everything about me. What I am going to do wrong, what I am going to do right, what I am going to choose in every moment. I ask that you would help me want to know you like you know me. You know more about me than I know about myself because you created me.

Father, if you know me so well, why should I ever be dishonest toward you? I want to be open with you even though you already know me so well. There isn't anything I can hide from you. You know what I need; knowing that makes me want to trust you completely.

Does God's intimate knowledge of you bring you comfort?

Joyful Surrender

*"All authority in heaven and on earth
has been given to me."*
MATTHEW 28:18 NIV

Jesus, I ask that you would help me surrender each day to you. I get carried away with little things and I become distracted with so many things throughout the day. Through all of that I want my focus to be toward you and on strengthening my faith in you. You have authority over every situation and only you can change anything.

God, not only do you control life on earth but you also control the heavens. When I am worried about something so little, I remember all that you do and I am amazed. Why do you do so much for me? I am so grateful for your love and how you care about everything in my life.

What can you surrender to God today?

CFW

July

Do not worry about anything,
but pray and ask God for everything
you need, always giving thanks.
And God's peace, which is so great
we cannot understand it, will keep
your hearts and minds in Christ Jesus.

Philippians 4:6-7 NCV

Delete Criticism

Do not let any unwholesome talk come out of your mouths,
but only what is helpful for building others up according
to their needs, that it may benefit those who listen.

EPHESIANS 4:29 NIV

Father, I know that sometimes I let words come out of my
mouth that I don't mean. I ask for your forgiveness. Other
times I say things I do mean and I know that it is wrong.
I ask that you would help me to be better at not being
quick to judge but easy to forgive and forget. Sometimes I
use words that I know are sinful and would upset people,
and I want to be better about that.

God, I want to show others your love by using kind words
even when they aren't around. That feels so much more
worth it than using words that offend. Sometimes other
people are saying something about someone else and
I ask that you would give me the strength to stop those
conversations and speak up for others.

How often do you spend your time criticizing people
when talking about them?

CFW

Your Reasons

Every person's way is right in his own eyes,
But the LORD examines the hearts.
PROVERBS 21:2 NASB

Father, I don't know how to explain my reasoning for some things, but you know my heart. You know why I said something a certain way or did something another way. You will judge my heart because you know what I intended. Sometimes I try to justify my own actions but instead I ask that you would assist me to stay strong and let myself be open with you.

God, there is no reason to hide my heart from you. I have a hard time letting go of things and letting other people be right or letting them do something their way. Show me how to let go and let you take control of my decisions and my life.

Do you ever stop to think about what the motivations of your heart are when you're on autopilot?

CFW

While I Wait

They desire a better, that is, a heavenly country.
Therefore God is not ashamed to be called their God,
for He has prepared a city for them.
HEBREWS 11:16 NKJV

Jesus, I am so thankful for the earth that you created. It is beautiful. While I wait for you, I ask that you would help me try my best to keep the earth like you made it. I am excited for the day that you will arrive on earth. I know that I will have to wait for that day to come, but I want to serve you while I do.

I thank you for all the things you put on earth to show your love for me. The oceans, the food, the people, and so much more. I am grateful for all of it, but I am more grateful for you. Thank you for your devotion to me and for creating something so great for everyone.

How do you deal with having to wait for something?

Freedom in Truth

"Then you will know the truth,
and the truth will make you free."
JOHN 8:32 NCV

God, I know that you are my freedom because your Word is the truth. Although I have felt obligated to do something, I ask that you would take that feeling away. I don't want any action done for you to feel like an obligation. I want to do something out of goodness and love for others.

Father, I know that your way is the truth and I pray that I do not stray from this truth. Sometimes when I am wrongfully accused and I know the truth, I want others to know it as well. But I don't need to convince anyone of anything because you know what is true and that is all that matters.

Are there any areas that you feel bound by obligation instead of freedom?

CFW

Simple Devotion

I'm afraid that just as Eve was deceived by the serpent's clever lies, your thoughts may be corrupted and you may lose your single-hearted devotion and pure love for Christ.

2 CORINTHIANS 11:3 TPT

God, I know that there are times when I have been deceived and corrupted. But I know that if I have your strength in me, I won't fail. With you, anything is possible. Although the devil may try to overtake me, I believe in your Son, Jesus, and he is stronger than any lie or deceit that is being thrown my way.

Lord, when my faith is weak and I fall, I stand back up again because of your grace and your truth. I never want to lose that feeling. When I love something or I have idols, it is harder for me to solely love you. I pray that you would destroy those feelings and help me to stay devoted to you.

What has distracted you from God's love lately?

CFW

A Season

For everything there is a season,
and a time for every matter under heaven:
ECCLESIASTES 3:1 NRSV

I believe that there are reasons for why things happen. It may be a lesson or something that is meant to be in my life. But you, Lord, put that in my life so that I would draw closer to you. I know that there are seasons where my faith wavers or where my faith is stronger than it ever has been before. I pray that when I sense either of these feelings, I would change things in my life and draw even closer to you.

Father, help me show this to other believers as well. Sometimes it is hard for people to remember that there is more to live for, but you are right there. You are the more that I want to live for.

Do you sense what type of spiritual season you're in?

Not Defeated

Every child of God defeats this evil world,
and we achieve this victory through our faith.

1 JOHN 5:4 NLT

God, every battle I have won, I have won through you.
This lesson is very important to remember. It is always
you that is there for me when I don't have anything else.
I know that you are what remains. Even if I have felt
defeated, I know that I am not alone, and I want to try
again.

I pray that my faith would grow stronger and that I
wouldn't chase after sin but that I would crush it when it
comes my way. I need you, Jesus. I don't know where I
would be without you, and I don't want to know. You have
given me stability and power every day of my life to walk
away from sin.

What areas of feeling defeated can you invite the Lord
into today?

CFW

Heartfelt Advice

Perfume and incense bring joy to the heart,
and the pleasantness of a friend
springs from their heartfelt advice.

PROVERBS 27:9 NIV

God, I am thankful for my friends. I know that you have placed each and every one of them in my life. I ask that you would help me be a light to my friends who do not know you. I want to be a friend that someone can go to without feeling judged and know they can be open with me about anything. Just like you do for me.

Lord, I am very grateful for the friends that have taught me more about you and for the ones that have taught me how to be like you. Not only am I grateful for friends that are believers, but I am happy that I have friends who aren't because it gives me someone to share the wonders of you with.

What is it like when you are around your closest friends?

Whatever I Ask

"If in my name you ask me for anything,
I will do it."
JOHN 14:14 NRSV

Father, you are so kind and caring. There isn't anything you don't know. I am glad that I can ask you anything and you know the answer. I pray that I will seek your answer before others. I know that sometimes I think my way is right or that someone who thinks a certain way is wrong, but I ask that you help me to search for you before others.

I don't want to hold back from asking something of you, but sometimes I feel as though I ask too much. From time to time, I wonder if I will get an answer from you, but if my faith is strong and my heart is strong for you, you will answer. You always do.

What have you held back from asking God?

CFW

My Need

Even lions may get weak and hungry,
but those who look to the LORD will have every good thing.
PSALM 34:10 NCV

God, you are always there for my needs. You provide
me with everything I need to live. I do not need to worry
because I know that you will be here for me. I have fallen
into temptation and although it is hard not to, waiting and
following you is so much better.

God, at times I worry that I won't get what I want, but if I
am patient and wait for you, you will give me what I need
and more. I ask that you strengthen my patience for you.
Help me to wait for the answer that you have for me
because I know that what you have in store is worth all of
my patience.

What do you need today?

CFW

Bearing Gifts

There are varieties of gifts, but the same Spirit. And there are varieties of ministries, and the same Lord. There are varieties of effects, but the same God who works all things in all persons. But to each one is given the manifestation of the Spirit for the common good.

1 CORINTHIANS 12:4-7 NASB

Jesus, I am so thankful for the gifts you have given me, even the ones I don't know of yet. I am excited to share these gifts with those who don't follow you. I pray that you would guide me and teach me the best ways to use the gifts you have given me. I know that each person on this earth is unique because you made every one of us yourself and we are all different.

Father, I ask that you would help me explore my gifts but show others that they have gifts of their own. Although everyone is different, we each use our gifts to praise you. Please remind me to use my gifts only for you.

What gifts has God put in you to reflect his character to others?

Beloved Child

You are altogether beautiful, my love;
there is no flaw in you.
SONG OF SOLOMON 4:7 ESV

Jesus, sometimes I have a hard time loving myself. I think that there are things wrong with me. I look at myself and I don't like what I see. Why do you not see any of that? I want to be confident and love myself and I know that I need you to do that.

Father, when I see that you think I am beautiful, I feel comforted. Someone who knows everything about me, the bad and the good, sees me as having no flaws. I don't understand how after you have seen the worst in me, you still believe that I am beautiful. Thank you for loving me even when I don't believe I deserve it.

What does it mean for you to know that you are a beloved child of the King?

CFW

Sadness

Cast all your anxiety on him,
because he cares for you.
1 PETER 5:7 NRSV

Father, there is so much anxiety in this world. When I think about something too often, or when my day is very busy and I'm worried about the outcomes of so many things, I pray that I would turn to you. You are what will guide me through this anxiety.

Jesus, you take care of all my emotions. If I turn to you, you are there to take care of me and my needs. When I am hurt and I think there is nothing left for me, I think about you and how I can share an eternity with you. Something that seems so big in my life is just another problem that won't matter in the long run.

What weighty emotions can you offer God today?

CFW

Beautiful Future

> "No eye has seen, no ear has heard,
> and no mind has imagined
> what God has prepared
> for those who love him."
>
> 1 CORINTHIANS 2:9 NLT

Lord, sometimes I wonder what the future will look like. I think about how small things are now compared to what will happen later on. I can't even imagine how miraculous an eternity in your kingdom will be. Sometimes I worry about how everything is going to be so different. But I know that you will be there and you will guide me.

Father, you created life on earth and you already have something much greater in store for me. I am excited to spend the rest of my days with you. Help me to glorify your name before these days come.

Do you feel hope or dread for the future?

CFW

Not Neglected

He will care for the needy and neglected
when they cry to him for help.
The humble and helpless will know his kindness,
for with a father's compassion he will save their souls.
PSALM 72:12-13 TPT

Father God, you love everyone no matter what they have done. How is that possible? You care for everyone like they mean the world to you. When anyone runs to you, they are immediately accepted and you care for them because they are your child.

Jesus, I ask that I would do the same for those who come to me. Help me look at them like they are just as important as anyone else. I want to show how much you love everyone through my actions. If I show love to those who need it, they will know what it is like to be in a relationship with you. I pray that this would be something I want to do for the rest of my life.

Who can you speak up for?

Forever Obedience

I will keep on obeying your instructions
forever and ever.
PSALM 119:44 NLT

Lord, I know that it is important to follow what you tell me. When I look away from these things, I learn that I should've followed what I heard you say and what I knew was right. Remind me that your words are more important than any other words I might start to believe. If I hear you tell me what is right, I want to follow what you say.

God, the instructions you have for me are to prepare me to spend my life with you, and I want to be a delight to you. I pray that you would help me make a clear distinction from what I think I hear you say and what I know you are telling me.

What has the Lord been nudging you toward?

CFW

No Dread

"Be strong and bold; have no fear or dread of them,
because it is the LORD your God who goes with you;
he will not fail you or forsake you."
DEUTERONOMY 31:6 NRSV

Father, sometimes I dread doing things that fall outside of what I want. I know that I should be more open and should be more willing to do things that are important to you and to people that I love. I know that you won't fail me. You are the one thing I can always depend on.

God, I pray that I would guard my heart and mind from things that keep me away from you. There are things that are hard for me to do on my own, and when I try to do everything myself, I fail. When I ask for your help, I succeed. I don't need to do things on my own because you are always with me.

What battle feels too large to face on your own?

CFW

Greatest Blessing

"The LORD bless you and keep you;
the LORD make his face shine on you and be gracious to you;
the LORD turn his face toward you and give you peace."

NUMBERS 6:24-26 NIV

God, you are my greatest blessing. You have blessed me with life and love. You provide me with peace and comfort. No one can do the same. There hasn't been a day where you haven't loved me or cared about me. I want to fall more in love with you. I want to spend more time with you. I want you to be my priority.

I don't want to turn away from you any longer. I want my heart to be open toward you. Sometimes I forget that I don't just want these things, I need them. I need you, Jesus. You have blessed me with so much in this life and I know that sometimes I forget that, but I am very thankful for all you have done for me.

What blessings are you thankful for today?

Heavenly Desires

Think about the things of heaven,
not the things of earth.
COLOSSIANS 3:2 NLT

God, I get caught up in this world. I pay attention to things or people more than you. I should be thinking about the future and about my time with you. Yet, I look at things that have hurt me or things that have changed me. I pray that you would keep me strong and that I would long for you.

Lord, the earth is full of evil and temptation. But I want to spend time with you and ignore the things of this world. Help me to put heavenly values before the values here. The time I devote to praising you means so much more than falling into sin here on earth.

What heavenly values do you think most about?

CFW

A Giving Heart

In all things I have shown you that by working hard in this way we must help the weak and remember the words of the Lord Jesus, how he himself said, "It is more blessed to give than to receive."

ACTS 20:35 ESV

Father, I ask that you help me to give more than I receive. Most importantly, I ask that you help me want to give things that mean a lot to me. It is easy to give things that I don't care for or don't want, but it is hard to give things up that I really want or use often.

God, I pray that I would notice what these things are and that it would be easy for me to give them up especially for someone I might not want to give them to. I ask that you not only help me give up materialistic things but also things like time and love.

What can you give away more of on a regular basis?

CFW

A Needed Helper

"The Helper, the Holy Spirit whom the Father will send in My name, He will teach you all things, and remind you of all that I said to you."

JOHN 14:26 NASB

Jesus, there are so many things that are incredible about you. There is more than one way for me to feel connected to you and there are so many ways I can praise your name. The Holy Spirit is inside of me and is always with me. Whenever I need you, I realize that the Holy Spirit is already there.

God, there are so many wonders that you do for me. You sent the Holy Spirit to fill the dead souls on this earth and bring them to life. I am so grateful that you chose me to be a part of your kingdom. Your Holy Spirit reminds me that you are always a passion inside of me.

How do you see the work of the Holy Spirit in your life?

CFW

Persistent Problems

I begged the Lord three times
to take this problem away from me.
2 CORINTHIANS 12:8 NCV

God, although there are problems I have where I ask you to help me, sometimes I learn that there was a reason why you didn't solve the problem right away. I know that in the end you will help me overcome any problems I might run into.

Although there are situations where I might feel weary and get tired of asking for help, Lord, I pray that I wouldn't stop. I know that asking over and over again is sometimes the answer, but what I need to learn is that I am not alone and that an answer to my problem will come. So, I ask for patience while I wait for those answers.

Is there a struggle that is hard for you to shake?

CFW

Surrender Again

My child, give me your heart,
and let your eyes observe my ways.
PROVERBS 23:26 NRSV

Lord, every day I have to surrender my heart to you. Sometimes I forget that, and I feel like I've lost you. But I can't lose you. I can lose myself. I don't want to lose myself anymore, Jesus.

I want to be faithful to you and I want to remember all that you do for me. I want to look at all that you do and I want to be like you. You are so kind, gentle, peaceful, and compassionate. I want to be an example of you to those who need to see what you are like. I can surrender anything to you without fear; show me how to surrender my heart completely to you. I want to set my heart on you and not on other people.

What can you lay on the altar of surrender?

CFW

Moved with Compassion

Jesus, when He came out, saw a great multitude and was moved with compassion for them, because they were like sheep not having a shepherd. So He began to teach them many things.
MARK 6:34 NKJV

Jesus, it is so wondrous to see that you have emotions like I do. You were moved when you saw that people needed someone to guide them and you chose to be a leader. You had compassion for all of these people and you knew each and every one of them. Even if they were going to betray you or they had done something terrible, you cared for them.

Jesus, I ask that I would be more like that. I want to be able to care for people even when they hurt me, and I want to be compassionate without judging those who have done things they regret. I pray that while I try to do this for others, I would teach them to do the same.

When was the last time compassion moved you to do something?

CFW

Resource of Hope

Encourage the hearts of your fellow believers
and support one another, just as you have already been doing.

1 THESSALONIANS 5:11 TPT

Father God, when people are connected through you, they don't need other things to keep them content. Sometimes it is hard for me to continuously choose you even when I am with other believers. I know that it's wrong, but I want to change. When I am with my friends that are believers, we talk about you but not as much as we talk about other things.

Lord, I ask that you would help me to stick to your Word and support my Christian friends in doing things for you. I want to be someone that is an example of your love and I want to encourage other believers to do the same.

How does being with other believers strengthen your hope in the Lord?

CFW

Gift of Grace

By grace you have been saved through faith;
and this is not of yourselves, it is the gift of God;
not a result of works, so that no one may boast.
EPHESIANS 2:8-9 NASB

Father, help me to be strong but not proud. I don't want to boast about what I have or how strong my faith is for you. I just want to share your love with others. Being boastful can push people away instead of drawing them close.

God, your grace is what saved me. I have never known anyone so full of grace. I pray that you would help me have grace like yours for others. I haven't saved myself; it was you that saved me. I am now clean and pure because of your forgiveness. Please use me to guide others to the same grace you gave me.

Are you confident that God's love covers every one of your weaknesses?

Joyful Hope

Be joyful because you have hope.
Be patient when trouble comes, and pray at all times.
ROMANS 12:12 NCV

Jesus, show me what it is like to be patient. When things come my way that trouble me, I want to fix it right away or change something so that it's no longer affecting me. Give me the strength I need to persevere through those times. I pray that I would be a delight. I want to be joyful because I am full of the Holy Spirit. I want people to see me as someone who is hopeful and happy because your love is inside of me.

Mostly God, I want to be reminded to look to you at all times. When life throws challenges my way and I am unhappy, I pray and ask for your help the most. But I want to ask for your help at all times and continuously talk to you. What is a relationship with someone if you don't spend time with them?

Where does your hope come from?

Compared to Glory

I consider that our present sufferings are not worth comparing with the glory that will be revealed in us.
ROMANS 8:18 NIV

Jesus, when something happens in my life, I think about it a lot. I think about how I could have done something differently or how I could have changed a situation. But these problems that are so big to me now won't matter to me when I am in your kingdom or even in the near future. What is more important is glorifying you and your Word before other things.

Father, I ask that you would remind me of this when I am stressed or when a problem comes into my life that I feel like I will never solve. The glory that you have is so much greater than any problem in my life, and I thank you for showing me that.

What happens to your heart and hopes in suffering?

CFW

Turn Away

No temptation has overtaken you except such as is common to man; but God is faithful, who will not allow you to be tempted beyond what you are able, but with the temptation will also make the way of escape, that you may be able to bear it.

1 CORINTHIANS 10:13 NKJV

Lord, evils in this world tempt me every day. There are things that I want or think I deserve, but I am wrong. When I think of you and what you would want me to do, it is easier for me to stop myself from falling into temptation. Thank you for keeping certain temptations away from me, but also thank you for giving me the strength I need to say no.

God, there have been times where I have fallen into temptation over and over again, but I know that if I ask you to help me, you will. When I have failed and have given in to temptation, I am able to get back up again because of you.

When you are tempted, what tools keep you from giving in?

CFW

When Plans Change

This change of plans greatly upset Jonah,
and he became very angry.
JONAH 4:1 NLT

God, when I am excited about something and all of the sudden things are cancelled or someone changes the plans, it's hard for me to not be upset. I know that there are reasons for a plan changing. Maybe it was another way of drawing me close to you, or a way of protecting me from something.

Jesus, sometimes I forget to see it this way and I get angry, but I pray that whatever plan was changed will draw me closer to you. I know that it is harder especially when plans I had were with someone I really wanted to spend my time with, but I pray that my heart would be drawn to you and you would be the one I want to spend my time with.

How do you react when your plans are changed?

With Endurance

Since we are surrounded by so great a cloud of witnesses,
let us also lay aside every weight, and sin which clings so closely,
and let us run with endurance the race that is set before us.
HEBREWS 12:1 ESV

Jesus, there are a lot of sins that try to keep me from you. I can feel when I am loosening my grip on you. There are people who know what sins I have committed, but I pray that I would be able to be open with those who can encourage me instead of drawing them into the same sin.

Some people in my life encourage my sin as well, which makes it harder to stay away from it. I ask that I would spend more time with you and people who want me to do good by you. I want to have endurance for you at all times during my life especially when I am trapped in sin and temptation.

What is weighing you down and holding you back as you journey through this life?

CFW

August

Trust the LORD with all your heart,
and don't depend
on your own understanding.
Remember the LORD in all you do,
and he will give you success.

PROVERBS 3:5-6 NCV

What You Want

"Father, if you are willing, take away this cup of suffering.
But do what you want, not what I want."

LUKE 22:42 NCV

Lord, I ask that when you take away my sins you would change something in my life, so I can be a greater example of you. I know there are ways that I can better myself for you and others. I ask that you would give me the perseverance to do this.

Father, there are so many ways that you lead me, but help me to follow. I know that I can wander away but you are my shepherd and I want to follow you. I ask that you would remind me of what I learned from my suffering. There are many times where I didn't ask for your help because I thought my way was right, but I learned that following your footsteps is so much more important.

Are you resisting the Lord's leadership in any area of your life?

Hidden Pain

Heal me, LORD, and I will be healed;
Save me and I will be saved,
For You are my praise.
JEREMIAH 17:14 NASB

Father, sometimes I am afraid to let you into the pain I am hiding. I am afraid to be so vulnerable with someone because I have before and I lost that connection many times. But you know me so well, and you won't forsake me. I ask that I would learn how to be vulnerable and open with you, and I ask that you would teach me to guard my heart from other things and save it for you.

God, you already know the pain hidden inside of me, so why do I hide? Please teach me to stay away from hiding my heart. If I let you into my heart you will protect me and be faithful. Thank you.

Will you let God into your hidden pain?

CFW

With Patience

If we hope for what we do not see,
we wait for it with patience.
ROMANS 8:25 NRSV

Father, you know my patience. You know that sometimes I am weak. I have a hard time waiting. But I want to wait for you because I want to be in your presence. I want to know you and I can't wait for the day that you come down to earth. It is harder to believe in things that you can't see. Lord, I have felt you in my life and I know that you are there. I am sorry for questioning your faithfulness. I ask that you would strengthen my patience and keep me determined to know you and to tell others about your wonders. I have hope for the day you come to earth and I get to spend eternity with you. I am so excited, Jesus.

What do you do when your patience is running thin?

CFW

Crown of Life

Blessed is the one who perseveres under trial because,
having stood the test, that person will receive the crown of life
that the Lord has promised to those who love him.

JAMES 1:12 NIV

Lord, I ask that I would persevere with you throughout my life. I am worried that I will lose my heart for you. Please strengthen me in this. I want to love you with all of my heart, and the best way for me to do that is to keep my heart only for you until I am ready to share it with another. I don't know how to love people if it isn't with your love.

God, please remind me that the best way to persevere is to spend as much time as I can with you. When my trial comes, I want to be able to confess what I have done wrong without worry. I want to be able to look at you and not be ashamed because you will know exactly what my heart feels.

What do you need today to keep persevering in areas that you've been losing strength?

CFW

My Dreams

Take delight in the LORD,
and he will give you the desires of your heart.

PSALM 37:4 NRSV

God, sometimes it is hard for me to let go and dive into you. I want to delight in you, but sometimes I think that doing my own thing will make me happier. Then I realize that delighting in you is the only thing that can truly make me happy. Life without you just isn't life.

Father, I don't want the only reason I delight in you to be so that I can have the desires of my heart. There are so many things that I desire, but sometimes I look for them in the wrong place or without you. If I am following you, you will give me what I need. Lord, show me the best way to delight in you and keep me from going my own way.

What desires can you bring before God today, letting him share in both the longing and the dreaming?

CFW

As I love

> "To you who are willing to listen, I say, love your enemies!
> Do good to those who hate you. Bless those who curse you.
> Pray for those who hurt you."
> LUKE 6:27-28 NLT

Jesus, when someone has hurt me, I find it hard to love them. I want to be better at loving my enemies and I want to show that I love them. Sometimes the people who hurt others the most are people who are the most hurt. But when I am caught up in drama with someone like that, I forget how hard they might have it.

Father, I pray that you would help me be willing to love these people. They need to see what love is like and most of all they need to see what your love is like. I ask that you would give me the patience and grace I need to love well.

Can you choose to replace the hate in your heart with love or at least the willingness to love?

CFW

No Reason to Fear

God has not given us a spirit of fear,
but of power and of love and of a sound mind.
2 TIMOTHY 1:7 NKJV

God, when I am afraid, you help me and give me peace.
I am thankful for the fear in this world because it has
taught me how powerful you are and how much you love
me. I know that fear tries to destroy me, but when I look
to you, I gain confidence and I am so much greater than
that fear when I fight it with you.

Jesus, when I am troubled and I say your name, I feel
peace immediately wash over me. I pray that I would
continuously go to you when times are hard, because
you give me power and love to overcome all the fear
clouding my judgment.

When fear intimidates you, how do you combat it?

CFW

A Silent Fight

"The LORD will fight for you,
and you have only to be silent."
EXODUS 14:14 ESV

God, when there are things that come to destroy my faith, I know that I can depend on you, and you can help me through the battle. I don't have to fight every battle on my own because I have you to guard me. There is nothing that you can't defeat. If I give my problems to you, they will be handled.

Father, I pray that I wouldn't try to do everything on my own; instead, I would run straight to you and ask for help with my troubles. Any fight without you is impossible. Jesus, I forget how much you do for me. Sometimes I don't understand why, but you do things anyway. Help me do the same for others.

Can you let God into the place of defending you instead of trying to do it on your own?

CFW

Perfect Peace

You will keep in perfect peace
all who trust in you,
all whose thoughts are fixed on you!
ISAIAH 26:3 NLT

Father, if I am constantly spending time with you, I feel the same peace throughout that time. I know that sometimes I am weak but I have never forgotten the peace that you bring me. I ask that you would show me what it feels like to trust in your name. I am sorry for where my thoughts have wandered.

God, I know that I have thought of things that were unclean and I haven't always kept my thoughts fixed on you. But I want to remember to do this every day. If my mind and my heart is toward you, my life will be full of peace and comfort because you stay true to your Word and you know what is best for me.

Where does your trust lie?

CFW

Growing Wiser

The wisdom from above is always pure, filled with peace,
considerate and teachable. It is filled with love and never displays
prejudice or hypocrisy in any form.

JAMES 3:17 TPT

Father, I know you are not a hypocrite. But sometimes
I am. I do something that I know is wrong but then I
criticize another person when they committed the same
sin. Assist me in this, Jesus. I should keep to myself or
help someone who has sinned in the same way I have.

God, I don't want people to feel judged by me. I want to
have an open heart for you and for people who need to
see your love. You are open-minded and you know what
my heart desires. I know that your wisdom is what I need
to hear and what I should follow. I pray that I would learn
to be like you in the same way.

What does wisdom look like in your life?

CFW

Flaming Darts

*In all circumstances take up the shield of faith,
with which you can extinguish all the flaming darts of the evil one.*
EPHESIANS 6:16 ESV

God, the devil tries to take my faith away, but you are stronger. And with you I am stronger than the temptation and sin that might be sent my way. I ask that my faith would grow so deep that I would want to continuously pick myself back up. I pray that my faith in you won't ever stop growing.

Father, I want to spend an eternity with you. The devil has tempted me and I have fallen into those temptations many times. I pray that when I fall, I would repent and I would grow stronger in you. Let my thoughts not stray far from you but help them to stick with you.

What does your faith provide you with today?

CFW

Burning Joy

"Go your way, eat the fat and drink sweet wine
and send portions of them to those for whom nothing is prepared,
for this day is holy to our LORD; and do not be grieved,
for the joy of the LORD is your strength."

NEHEMIAH 8:10 NRSV

Father, I want to thank you for the blessing that I receive from you each day. You bring me so much joy and I know that you are what I need to stay strong. You want me to be happy in my life and you want me to share this joy with others and with you. I know that I can never fully be content without you.

God, I can't explain the joy that you give me, but it is unmatchable. I want each day to be holy to you. When I am filled with joy from you, I am stronger than ever because my faith in you is determined and I have set my ways to you. I ask that you would help me want that joy to burn inside me for the rest of my days.

Which characteristic of God brings you joy today?

CFW

With Everything

"You will seek me and find me
when you seek me with all your heart."

JEREMIAH 29:13 NIV

God, when I give you everything, I find myself so close
to you. It is harder to see what you are like when I don't
want to look for you with everything I have. The times
that I have felt weary and ran to you, I received your love.
I want to seek you with everything.

Father, I ask you to clear my mind and only search for
you. When I do this, all of my desires and thoughts will be
solved because you take care of me. I am so grateful for
your devotion to my needs. I want to be devoted to you.
Help me to be honest with you and show you where my
heart is.

Will you be honest with where your heart is today?

CFW

Give More

"If anyone slaps you on one cheek,
offer him the other cheek, too.
If someone takes your coat,
do not stop him from taking your shirt."

LUKE 6:29 NCV

Lord, teach me how I can give more. There are so many things I could give to others and to you. Show me what those things are so that I can continuously give for you. Sometimes when I have something that is important to me, I don't want to give it up. But if that is what I need to do, then you will guide me through that and I will follow.

God, if someone betrays me and they hurt me, you tell me to give to them anyway. Sometimes these lessons you give me are hard to follow, but I know that I will not be shaken if I am following you.

Do you assert your rights over others, or do you follow Jesus' humble example?

CFW

Called Out

You are a chosen generation, a royal priesthood, a holy nation,
His own special people, that you may proclaim the praises of Him
who called you out of darkness into His marvelous light.
1 PETER 2:9 NKJV

Jesus there is a reason for why you called me into your truth. You chose me for a greater purpose. As thankful as I am, I don't understand why. Why would you choose someone who you knew would question your Word?

Father, I ask that you would teach me how I can be a greater servant to you and show me the reasons for why you have chosen me. Use me as a light that guides people into your truth. Not only have you chosen me, but you chose others to show your love as well. Keep me close to these people so together we can share your Word. Thank you for choosing me.

What is the driving force of your life?

Equal Trust

Be strong and courageous,
all you who put your hope in the LORD!
PSALM 31:24 NLT

Jesus, it's hard for me to trust. I have been broken in the past. You are the only one who can fix me and heal me with love. I don't know how to be strong without you. I pray that through all of this, you would strengthen my trust toward you and toward others.

God, if I trust in you, I shouldn't need to trust other people. But I pray that you would make me want to try because trust is important to have in any relationship. I know that I can trust you to take care of my life. Whether it's my faith or something I need, you are always dependable. My hope is in you.

Do you trust God to take care of you?

CFW

With Help

I will instruct you and teach you the way you should go;
I will counsel you with my eye upon you.
PSALM 32:8 NRSV

God, I know that there is always more for me to learn from you. You have taught me so much already, but there is so much more for me to know. I pray that you would remind me of what I can do to be teachable. If I am stubborn and try things my own way, I never get anywhere.

Jesus, I need direction in my life and you know where to lead me. You are the one person I can truly depend on and you are the only one I can trust my life with. Show me how to best follow you and help me to guide others to you as well.

What do you need direction for right now?

CFW

Hope Wins

We also have joy with our troubles, because we know that these troubles produce patience. And patience produces character, and character produces hope.

ROMANS 5:3-4 NCV

Jesus, you help me learn from my troubles. I know that every challenge I face is a lesson you want to teach me. With your love, I always get back up. There is joy that comes from my troubles, but it takes time. The joy I have felt comes after I learn the lesson.

God, sometimes I forget how to have hope for certain things because I have been hurt over and over. But you give me hope for the future and hope for an eternal life in your kingdom. I thank you for everything you have put in my life because I know that there was a purpose for each thing.

Where do you see the fruit of hope in your life?

CFW

Rest Awhile

All who have entered into God's rest have rested from their labors, just as God did after creating the world.

HEBREWS 4:10 NLT

Father, I know that resting is important, but sometimes I am so busy I forget to rest. There is so much peace in resting for a day. I am thankful for that peace from you. I ask that I would remember to take a day of rest so that I can be refreshed in you. I also ask that I would use my day of rest to listen to your Word and devote that time to you.

God, it is important for me to sit back and appreciate the things in my life that mean the most to me. I am thankful for everything you have given me, and I am also thankful that I can rest in your presence and feel peace when I am with you.

When was the last time you spent a whole day doing what was restful?

CFW

Reign Together

If we are joined with him in his sufferings,
then we will reign together with him in his triumph.
But if we disregard him, then he will also disregard us.
2 TIMOTHY 2:12 TPT

Jesus, you will reign over the heavens and the earth. I pray that you would help me speak your word to non-believers so they will join you in your kingdom. Help me build this kingdom with you. Help me to lead other believers around me to your Word so we can join together and praise your name.

Lord, I have hope for the day you return and destroy all of the sin and evil in this world. I ask that I would not disregard you or what you are trying to teach me. When I choose my own way, I fall deeper into sin and I regret not choosing your Word. I don't want to live like that.

What would it cost you to give up your faith?

CFW

Let Go

A time to seek, and a time to lose;
a time to keep, and a time to cast away.
ECCLESIASTES 3:6 NRSV

I look at the past and I wonder what went wrong. What did I do? I think of everything I could have done differently because I cared, and I still care. But God, I don't need to think of those times. Because I know that mistakes were made and I know things could have gone differently, but it doesn't matter because you are teaching me.

Father, you knew what was best for me and you made my life different. There are other things that have been constant in my life, which is also your doing. You know what is best for me, and I ask that you would remind me of that.

What do you need to let go of?

CFW

My Comforter

"Take my yoke upon you. Let me teach you,
because I am humble and gentle at heart,
and you will find rest for your souls."
MATTHEW 11:29 NLT

Jesus, I ask that you would teach me what it feels like to
be at peace even in troubled times. You are very caring
and trustworthy and I want to be the same to those
around me. When I am tired and weary, I want to run
to you and seek rest in you. I get carried away with my
thoughts and sometimes even my actions, but I want to
pay attention to what you have given me and what I need
most—you.

God, I keep searching for the one thing that could make
me feel peace and rest and I try everywhere, but I forget
to look at the one thing that has stayed constant in my
life. I ask that you would help me to look to you first.

Can you invite God into your pain, daring to see where
he is in it?

True Faithfulness

My covenant I will not break,
Nor alter the word that has gone out of My lips.
PSALM 89:34 NKJV

Father God, you have kept all of your promises to me, but I have not done the same for you. I have said I was going to do something or changed how I reacted to something, but I wasn't always true to my word. I am thankful that your Word is always true. I ask that you would help me to stay faithful to you and to stick to the words that come out of my mouth.

God, I don't want the words that I have promised you to mean any less to me when something changes or becomes more convenient. If I stay faithful to my word, I can be trustworthy with you and with other people in my life.

What promises of God are you standing on?

CFW

Abundance Stored

How abundant are the good things
that you have stored up for those who fear you,
that you bestow in the sight of all,
on those who take refuge in you.
PSALM 31:19 NIV

Jesus, the number of things you have given me in this life is incredible. You have blessed me with so much. I am sorry if I have ever taken what I have for granted. It is hard to forget how to be thankful when life is challenging, but I know that I am lucky because you are in it.

Father, you have given me blessings that I don't even know about. I know that even if I have lost sight of my faith, you are waiting for me to come running back into your arms. You don't fail me, and you never will. You take care of all of my needs and bless me with so much more.

What gifts has God deposited in your life that are pure goodness?

CFW

Protected Heart

Do not be fooled:
"Bad friends will ruin good habits."
1 CORINTHIANS 15:33 NCV

God, when I am with people who are non-believers I have a harder time following your ways. Although I want to be a light to these friends, sometimes it is better to stay away and keep to my Christian friends. I pray that I would see when my friends are influencing me negatively and when they are doing things out of your truth.

Lord, I ask that it would be easier to surround myself with people that want to do right by you. Some of the connections I have with friends are close, but they aren't as deep as the relationships I have with those who are faithful to you.

Who do you need to allow less access to your life?

CFW

Wise Counsel

Without consultation, plans are frustrated,
But with many counselors they succeed.
PROVERBS 15:22 NASB

Jesus, you have blessed my life with many leaders and followers. I ask that you would help me follow the truth and devote myself to you like other believers. When I am weak, I know that these people are the ones I can turn to.

Father, I ask that you would help me to be an example to others as well. I know that I have learned many things from you; help me share what I have learned with those who need to hear it. When I have ideas, help me feel comfortable sharing them with others so I can know whether it is an idea that will follow your ways or if it is something that could lead me into evil.

What plans have you been devising on your own that could benefit from outside perspective?

Words of Life

"I tell you, on the day of judgment you will have to give an account for every careless word you utter; for by your words you will be justified, and by your words you will be condemned."

MATTHEW 12:36-37 NRSV

Lord, I know there are times when I say things that I don't mean. But I pray that I will be wise. The words that I use matter because they have meaning. Words can have a million different meanings behind them, but you always know what I mean when I say them. Because you know my heart and mind.

Father, I pray that I will not be careless with my words but that I will mean everything I say. Words have a very strong impact on every situation. I want to speak loudly and truthfully about you. Help me devote my days on this earth to you so I am always ready to talk about my faith.

Do you consider the impact of your words before you speak them?

CFW

Healing Hearts

He heals the brokenhearted
and bandages their wounds.
PSALM 147:3 NLT

Father, sometimes I feel heartbroken, hurt, or upset. Even during trying times, I thank you that you are a healing God. Thank you for not just healing physical wounds, but emotional wounds too. I pray you comfort me when I am upset or struggling through heartbreak. Bring me peace that stills all disaster. Help me to lean on others who love you.

Lord, heal my heart and help me grow close to you in times of need. Encourage me to read your Word and talk to you often. Help me to find joy in worshipping and praising you even when I do not feel content. Thank you that you love me regardless of my faults or feelings. Thank you for your unconditional love that covers all fear and worry. I pray you lift me up and bring me joy.

Is there a heartbreak that you can invite the Lord into?

CJW

Intuition

Do not believe every spirit, but test the spirits, whether they are of God; because many false prophets have gone out into the world.

1 JOHN 4:1 NKJV

As I reflect on my relationship with you, I know I can always trust you and your Word. Father, thank you for intuition and discernment. I know that through you, it is possible to know who a false prophet is. Give me sensitivity toward the Holy Spirit to feel when something is not from you. I pray you help me to learn and strengthen my discernment. Help me to tell the difference between false teachings and teachings from you.

God, give me the wisdom to search for and find the truth. Encourage me to use your Word to find the answer to what has been put into question. Through prayer and verses from the Bible, I ask the Holy Spirit to be upon me when I am feeling unsure or uneasy. Give me clarity to seek out the truth and be with me always.

Do you trust that you are able to test whether a teaching is from God or not?

CJW

For Good

We are convinced that every detail of our lives is continually woven together to fit into God's perfect plan of bringing good into our lives, for we are his lovers who have been called to fulfill his designed purpose.

ROMANS 8:28 TPT

Lord, you know everything that has happened in my life and that will happen in my future. Thank you that you are all-knowing and wise. It is because of your plan that I do not need to worry about my future or what might happen. Thank you for your peace that surpasses all understanding! Thank you for your love that casts away all anxieties.

Father, you give good things to those who serve you. Encourage me to draw near to you and follow you closely all the days of my life. Please give me wisdom in situations I face that I do not understand. Help me to find purpose in my life. Through this I know I will accomplish all you plan for me. Guide me to use the gifts you have given me. Please use these to bless those around me.

Looking at the bigger picture of your life, do you see the thread of God's goodness?

CJW

My Intercessor

In the same way the Spirit also helps our weakness;
for we do not know what to pray for as we should, but the Spirit
Himself intercedes for us with groanings too deep for words.
ROMANS 8:26 NASB

Thank you, Lord, for the Holy Spirit. Whenever I am too afraid or upset to speak, the Holy Spirit speaks to you for me. How incredible to serve a God that knows all things, even if I do not speak them aloud. Thank you for hearing every fear and understanding exactly what is wrong. I am so glad you are there always to comfort me.

Father, I ask that through the challenges I face, you encourage me to spend time with you. Even if I don't feel I can speak, I know your presence will uplift me and give me peace. I pray the Holy Spirit will be close to me always, interceding for me during worship or prayer. Help me to trust in the Holy Spirit to speak for me and through me when I am unable. Help me to know what to say or do in situations where I am unsure.

Do you trust that the Holy Spirit makes up the difference when you don't know what to say?

CSW

September

"Come to me,
all you who are weary and burdened,
and I will give you rest."

Matthew 11:28 niv

Making a Way

"Behold, I am doing a new thing;
now it springs forth, do you not perceive it?
I will make a way in the wilderness
and rivers in the desert."
ISAIAH 43:19 ESV

Jesus, I know that I go through different seasons throughout my life. Some are good and some are testing. Sometimes I feel close to you, others feel more distant. Sometimes my life seems intact and others it seems challenging. I pray that you be near me in all seasons. Please help me to seek after you and you only, Lord, no matter what may be distracting me.

I ask that you help me find joy in all seasons of life, even if I go through difficulty. Thank you for your joy, Jesus. I pray that I choose joy. Spending time with you encourages me and lifts my mood. Please remind me to praise you in the bad times as well as the good. Thank you that each season teaches me something different about myself. I pray each season, no matter what happens, brings me closer to you.

What new thing is God doing in your life?

CSW

Brave Honesty

Lying lips are an abomination to the LORD,
but those who act faithfully are his delight.
PROVERBS 12:22 NRSV

Father, sometimes lying seems more convenient than telling the truth. Help me to be brave in telling the truth! I know being deceitful can really hurt those close to me and it hurts you. I ask that you help me to speak the truth even when I struggle to. Even when I feel it will cost me or I might get into trouble. Before I choose to tell the truth or lie, help me to remember that you delight in those who speak the truth even in the difficult situations.

God, I want to be delighted in by you. Thank you that you see me as your child. Thank you for your forgiveness, and that you love me no matter what. I pray that when I make mistakes, I ask for forgiveness. I know you always forgive me when I ask, and for that, I am so grateful.

What does it cost you to be honest in hard situations?

CSW

Capable for Good

Using the Scriptures, the person who serves God will be capable, having all that is needed to do every good work.

2 TIMOTHY 3:17 NCV

Lord, you are a provider. Several times in the Bible you provided to those who served you. You ensured your people were taken care of. When I have a need, you fill it, sometimes without even being asked. You genuinely care for me and make sure I have all I need. Whether it is food, joy, or friendship, you provide.

Father, thank you for giving me everything I need to live and to better serve you. I know with you I will never be lacking in anything. If I feel I am lacking, I pray I draw near to you and seek your help. Thank you for always being near me and loving me unconditionally. I am so glad you are in my life. When I have you, I do not need anything else. I pray I always turn to you when I am unsure through prayer or worship.

When you don't know what to do, where do you turn?

CdW

The Right Path

A man's heart plans his way,
But the LORD directs his steps.
PROVERBS 16:9 NKJV

God, situations don't always go the way I plan or want them to. I find I might want to spend time with friends in the evening, but instead need to be home completing an assignment for school. This may be difficult, but I know that you have a purpose for each thing I experience. I ask that you teach me about what tasks should be prioritized and how to manage my time better.

Father, whether a situation goes my way or doesn't, I learn something, and I thank you for that. I pray that when it doesn't go as planned, you use it for your glory and teach me a lesson through it. Help me to accept whatever happens and talk to you if I feel let down. I know all lessons you display bring me closer to you and make me a better person. Thank you for all your teachings.

When things don't turn out the way you'd hoped, do you trust that the Lord has a plan?

CSW

Eternal Life

"God so loved the world that he gave his one and only Son, that whoever believes in him shall not perish but have eternal life."

JOHN 3:16 NIV

Father, I love verses like this that confirm just how much you love your children. Thank you for your Word that ministers to me. Thank you that the Bible has messages for every circumstance and every struggle. God, you loved us so much that you sent your only Son to us to suffer and die. No one has ever made such a sacrifice for those who are unworthy. I am blessed to follow you and be a part of your family.

Father, you allow those who choose you to be their life's focus to spend eternity with you. How beautiful it will be, being together forever with all who chose to follow you. Thank you for how much you love us, Father. Thank you for your unconditional love and everything you have done for me. Amen.

When you boil down your faith in Jesus to its simplest form, what does it look like?

CJW

Welcomed

Do not neglect to show hospitality to strangers,
for thereby some have entertained angels unawares.
HEBREWS 13:2 ESV

Jesus, I know that kindness is so important. I've felt how much it means when someone smiles at me or just says hello when I am having a tough day. I know you encourage kindness because it is one of the fruits of the Spirit, and that means it is of you.

Father, I ask that you help me to be kind to those who are kind to me, but also to my enemies. Your Word talks about the importance of praying for those who persecute or hurt me, and the importance of loving my enemies. Please help me to be kind even to my enemies and pray for them frequently. Encourage me to pray for them to get to know you and who you are. I pray my kindness to them brings them close to you. Please help heal my enemies. Show them the love only you can give.

When was the last time you showed kindness to a stranger?

Only Love

Love each other with genuine affection,
and take delight in honoring each other.
ROMANS 12:10 NLT

God, you have given me the capacity to love. Thank you for love that is unconditional, patient, kind, and conquers all fears and anxieties. I know if I feel doubt or hurt, all I need is you. I ask that you help me to love my neighbors, friends, and family. And especially, to love my enemies. It can be hard to love those who hurt me. Help me to love them and forgive as you do.

Father, remind me that you always offer forgiveness and I should do the same. Thank you that you created relationships and encourage me through them. I am so grateful for all the people who love you. Thank you for your love. I pray I focus my love on you and not on distractions that keep me from growing closer to you.

How does love honor others in your life?

CBW

More Like You

I pray with great faith for you, because I'm fully convinced that the One who began this glorious work in you will faithfully continue the process of maturing you and will put his finishing touches to it until the unveiling of our Lord Jesus Christ!

PHILIPPIANS 1:6 TPT

Father, thank you for growth. Thank you for the animals and plants that grow, and for personal growth. I may have started as someone with little faith, but I grew and can continue to grow and be more like you. I know you spent your time making me and you love me greatly. You made me unique and beautiful.

God, encourage me to learn about and exemplify the fruit of the Spirit. To love my neighbors and my enemies and pray for those who hurt me. Please encourage me to follow you closely all the days of my life. I want to be a light to all around me. Help me learn and obey your ways through these upcoming years. Draw me near to you and help me to live out your Word. Allow me to see the things I need to adjust to be more like you.

How do you see God's likeness showing up in you?

CJW

Adversity

"My grace is sufficient for you, for power is perfected in weakness." Most gladly, therefore, I will rather boast about my weaknesses, so that the power of Christ may dwell in me.
2 CORINTHIANS 12:9 NASB

Lord, I am not perfect. No one is perfect. No one beside you, Jesus. Please help me to remember I have faults and that those around me also make mistakes. Help me battle the anxiety of always getting the correct answer. Help me see that mistakes are made every day and that I should not be ashamed of these, but rather gain a lesson from them or ask for forgiveness. Mistakes teach us. Failure is important, just as practice is important.

Father, give me the strength to try again and again when I fail: to improve and push myself through challenges I face. Thank you that I can learn from mistakes and draw closer to you through them. If it's studying for a test, completing chores, or memorizing your Word, help me to practice and keep trying despite failing sometimes. Thank you that your strength pushes me forward and empowers me when I want to give up.

What weaknesses are areas in your life that God can empower with his strength?

CW

Love Never Ends

A thousand years in your sight
are like a day that has just gone by,
or like a watch in the night.

PSALM 90:4 NIV

God, thank you for you promises. They allow me to feel secure in you. I know you keep your promises to me. I know I can always trust you and that you'll love me forever. After a storm, I look into the sky and see a rainbow. I feel alive in moments like that. The rainbow reminds me of the promise you gave to your people about never flooding the earth again. I love the reminder of the promises you keep. It's such a beautiful sight.

Thank you, Lord, for other promises you've made me. Like the verse about you wiping away my fears and helping me. I'm so glad you are there for me. I know you'll never leave me alone. All I need to do is be still and trust you. Lord, you are so good to me. Thank you for your promises.

Does the timing of God's promises affect the love you feel from him?

CJW

The Same Hands

"You have also given me the shield of Your salvation;
your gentleness has made me great."
2 SAMUEL 22:36 NKJV

Father, I know you provide all I need. When I face trials, you love me unconditionally. When I make mistakes, you make me pure again. When I am weak, you are strong. When I think of a time I felt defeated, you were there, surrounding me, comforting me, and holding me.

Lord, thank you that you see my needs, emotions, and hardships. I'm so glad you don't sit on the sidelines. You heal me, bring restoration, and give me great gifts. You nourish me when I am weary. You care for me in a way that cannot be described. How incredible it is to be loved by you, Father. I pray that I try to love others the way you love me. I pray that I am a light to others in darkness. Help me to be compassionate and comforting. Help me to be more like you.

How does the use of your hands reflect the character of Christ?

CSW

No Words

They sat on the ground with him for seven days and seven nights. No one said a word to him, because they saw how great his suffering was.

JOB 2:13 NIV

Lord, you've taught me the importance of empathy to those around me, through your Word and the actions of those devoted to you. I know everyone has their struggles and challenges. Help me to remember the importance of the community of those who love you. I know I can lean on those you love you to help me through difficulties in my life.

Father, you gave me the ability to feel empathy and love, so I pray I use these to help those who are suffering. I know I don't ever need to be afraid to ask for help because I am not alone. Thank you that you fight my battles for me and you help me. You are always with me. Remind me to show empathy to those around me.

What do you do when those you love are suffering?

CJW

Victory

We thank God! He gives us the victory
through our Lord Jesus Christ.

1 CORINTHIANS 15:57 NCV

God, you are truly incredible! Throughout your Word, I
see that with your help, victory is achieved in battle—like
with David and Goliath. Victory can also be seen in the
people brought back to life and through those healed
from many diseases. Although these may not be the
types of victories I see in my life, if I think about it, a
victory for me may be getting an A on a test I studied for.
Thank you for all victories: big or small, they are made
possible by you. Through you, I know I can do all things.

Thank you, Father, that I can do all things through you. I
ask you to help me achieve victory in my life as you have
for many others who follow you. I am so grateful your
hand is over my life, sustaining and protecting me. Thank
you for blessing me and keeping me safe. Through you,
all things are possible.

What does the glory of victory in Jesus look like
in your life?

CZW

Brought Near

Bear one another's burdens,
and thereby fulfill the law of Christ.
GALATIANS 6:2 NASB

God, I know you are always with me. I am never alone. No matter what is happening around me, you are near. I pray I never forget that. You are with me. In times of doubt or fear, help me to remember those words. You are with me.

Father, when I am feeling low, encourage me to lean on my brothers and sisters in Christ. Whether I need comfort, clarity, or peace, I pray I remember to draw close to those who love you, so they can pray for me. Help me to be there for others who may ask for help from you. I pray to be an encouraging light to those in need. Thank you for uplifting me and drawing near to me. I am never truly alone, no matter how alone I may feel. Thank you for always having my back.

Who in your life helps you carry the weight of hard situations?

CSW

Good Discipline

If you do not punish your children, you don't love them,
but if you love your children, you will correct them.
PROVERBS 13:24 NCV

Lord, everyone gets in trouble sometimes; I know I do.
People make mistakes every day. Because of your Word,
I know that discipline is given by those who love me. By
those who want to help me learn important life lessons.
If they did not correct my mistakes, they would not be
showing me love.

Father, you discipline those you love so they can learn
from mistakes and become more like you. I pray that I
understand why I am being disciplined and do not hold
any anger in my heart. Help me to not be ashamed of my
mistakes but to be humble in the lessons I learn from my
errors. I pray for humility in my life. Encourage me to seek
out advice on how to become more like you from my
brothers and sisters in Christ. Thank you that I can learn
from my mistakes and become better for it.

Have you experienced God's discipline in your life?

CJW

Access to Wisdom

*"Call to me and I will answer you,
and will tell you great and hidden things
that you have not known."*
JEREMIAH 33:3 NRSV

Lord, you are faithful, loving, and all-knowing. You have many other characteristics that show just how amazing you are; you are truly incredible and wise beyond anything I can comprehend. You created all and watch over everything in the universe. I know you lead me in the right direction. Whenever I am confused or conflicted, I pray I call out to you. In times when I am not sure what to say or do, please lead me in your ways.

I want to live for you, God, and carry out your plan for my life and the lives I touch. I know you will answer my prayers and help me to make decisions. Father give me your wisdom when I feel lost. I know that will lead me onward. Thank you that you guide me in ways that further your plan for me. Thank you for making your wisdom accessible to me.

What do you need wisdom for today?

CSW

You Alone

No one is holy like the LORD!
There is no one besides you;
there is no Rock like our God.
1 SAMUEL 2:2 NLT

God, you are strong, mighty, and wise. You created everything in this world by speaking it into being. How incredible! You are stronger than anything I could imagine; you can carry the weight of the world so easily. For this reason, I know I can trust you with any aspect of my life. I know I never need to worry about the basic necessities of life because you provide.

Lord, you are my rock and my salvation. You keep me grounded in tough situations and make me feel uplifted. You save me from my sins and redeem me. You rescue me from challenges I face. I am so thankful the God I serve is so good. You are a good father to anyone who needs you. Thank you for the gift of your strength and salvation. Remind me that you are bigger than any of my life's problems. Remind me to draw close to you.

How can you practice shifting your perspective?

The Right Way

"I am the Way, I am the Truth, and I am the Life.
No one comes next to the Father except through union with me.
To know me is to know my Father too."

JOHN 14:6 TPT

God, you make my life better in so many ways. You provide for me when I am in need. You comfort me when I am at my lowest. You are my anchor. You build me up where I am weak. You are patient with me no matter what I have done, and you always forgive me. Your love never fails me. No one else in my life is like you.

Father, I am so blessed to be your child and to be part of your family. In times I need someone, whether it be a friend or father, I know I can count on you. I know you are there for me. It is an honor to serve you. I love you. Thank you for loving me too. Thank you for the way you created me and sustain me. I am forever grateful. You are the way, the truth, and the life.

How does knowing Jesus benefit your life?

CSW

Delight in Weakness

That is why, for Christ's sake, I delight in weaknesses,
in insults, in hardships, in persecutions, in difficulties.
For when I am weak, then I am strong.

2 CORINTHIANS 12:10 NIV

Father, sometimes it is difficult to find the positives, but thank you that there is always good in my life. I may feel challenged, but I know I will come through the difficulty with resistance and strength. It can be hard to love others who insult me or upset me; however, I know that through adversity I become stronger. When I draw close to you, you strengthen me. You are the stronghold in my life and you hold me together.

God, help me to see the good things that come from the bad, like the lessons I learn from my own weaknesses. This verse shows me that I should delight in the challenges I face, as I can learn from them. Help me to learn through hardships. Teach me to persevere through all difficulties. Build me up and strengthen me to better serve you.

Who do you turn to when you feel weak?

CSW

All Honor

The answer is, if you eat or drink, or if you do anything,
do it all for the glory of God.

1 CORINTHIANS 10:31 NCV

God, I want my life to glorify you always. Help me to
glorify you in the big and small. Whether it's doing the
dishes, driving the car, or taking a test, encourage me
to praise you though it all. I want to sing your praises
through the highs and lows of my life whenever possible.
I pray you have your hand over me, guiding my choices
and decisions.

Father, I know you are sovereign over every step of
my life. Please show me what you have in store for me
and what plan you have for my life. I want to honor you.
Remind me to praise you through all stages, seasons,
and situations that I go through. You deserve all the glory
because you are worthy.

Do you think about the mundane as opportunities to
glorify God?

CSW

Own Conscience

Whatever you believe about these things keep between yourself and God. Blessed is the one who does not condemn himself by what he approves.

ROMANS 14:22 NIV

Father, you are the best example of how someone should speak, act, and think. Thank you that I can look to you in any situation and receive clarity. I pray that I speak in the ways you do. I want to speak with kindness, love, and compassion. Help me to act in the ways you do. I want to act humbly and be diligent in any work I do.

Lastly, Lord, I want to think like you. Encourage my thoughts to be focused on you. Help me think kindly; I don't want to think poorly of others. Focus my mind on growing in faith. If I do this, I know that I will approve of righteous matters. Fuel my faith and draw me near to you. Encourage me to be more like you in every way.

What fuels your faith?

Powerful Presence

You make known to me the path of life;
in your presence there is fullness of joy;
at your right hand are pleasures forevermore.
PSALM 16:11 ESV

Father, thank you for the wonder of your joy that surpasses all understanding. It reminds me of the feeling you get when someone gives you a hug or surprises you with a gift, or of spending a beautiful day at a lake or beach. Your joy is so powerful. It can lift the feeling of depression or loss and it provides relief to those who are upset. When I've had a rough day or have felt unhappy, spending time with you alters my attitude and gets rid of any negativity.

Through prayer and worship I feel your presence, God, and I'm filled with joy. Your joy is pure. It brings a smile to my face and laughter that I cannot compare to any other feeling in the world. Thank you for the joy you give.

When is the last time you felt pure joy?

CSW

Life of Integrity

For our sake he made him to be sin who knew no sin,
so that in him we might become the righteousness of God.
2 CORINTHIANS 5:21 NRSV

Father, thank you for the sacrifice of your perfect Son, Jesus—the offering that led to the cleansing of all sins. He suffered greatly, so I could be with you forever. He died so I could live. What an incredible sacrifice. Thank you that the grave did not hold him and that he sits with you in heaven.

The grave has no power over me and I can grow in your righteousness, Jesus. I know integrity is so important. Build my integrity by showing me what in my life is of you and what needs to be changed. Help me to be honest, humble, and honorable. Strengthen me and teach me in these characteristics. Reveal to me what your plan is for my life. Revive me in your ways. Help me to live honorably.

What does living an honorable life mean to you?

CSW

Hated First

> "If the world hates you,
> remember that it hated me first."
> JOHN 15:18 NLT

Father, you created emotion and experienced it all. You felt every emotion long before I existed. You faced every challenge, hardship, and change. You were the first to see the seasons affect the weather and the plants. The first to feel heartbreak and anger. You experienced loss.

Thank you, Jesus, that you are engaging. You are easy to relate to because you experienced everything first. You went before me. You went through it all to know what it would be like for me. You felt all that pain so that I could live to know you and eventually stay with you in forever in heaven. I know I can ask you anything and I pray you give me wisdom to understand what I should do. Help me to lean on you in the challenges I face and to act humbly when those who don't like me challenge me or upset me. Thank you that you are such a caring God.

How do you react when people don't like you?

CSW

Greater Impact

Commit your work to the LORD,
and your plans will be established.
PROVERBS 16:3 NKJV

Thank you, Jesus, for your name that can change everything. When it's spoken, it allows people to feel loved, safe, and at peace. Just as those changes can happen, I know I am transformed by you. You have greatly impacted my life. Transform me in your light. Direct me in ways that will have an impact on those around me. Drench me in your glory and love.

Holy Spirit move in my life; I am ready for you to lead me. Encourage me to pray for those who do not know you. To show people the love you give your children. I know your love can break through all hearts and minds. Strengthen me and show me your plan for my life. I know your plan for me is good and will impact many lives that come across mine.

What do you want the impact of your life to be?

CSW

The Source

All praise to God, the Father of our Lord Jesus Christ.
God is our merciful Father and the source of all comfort.

2 CORINTHIANS 1:3 NLT

Father, you are the great comforter. You love me more deeply than anyone on earth could. You know my every need and want. I trust that you will care and provide for me. Thank you for your incomparable, unconditional love. You feel pain when I do, and you draw near to me. Your presence can move every mountain and solve any problem I face. Through you, all things are possible. No matter how down I feel, you light up the darkness in my life. Even when I feel hope is lost, with you, hope arises and breaks through all strongholds.

God, when I feel broken, pour out your love, comfort, and peace over me. Remind me to call on your name when I feel weak. Thank you that you make me strong in my weaknesses. Be the center of my focus and the source for every good thing in my life.

Do you believe that God has resources to meet every one of your needs?

CJW

Anchored

Let him ask in faith, with no doubting, for he who doubts is like a wave of the sea driven and tossed by the wind.

JAMES 1:6 NKJV

Lord, thank you for faith. I know faithfulness is one of the fruit of the Spirit and that if I am full of faith, I can accomplish anything through you. Remind me that nothing is impossible with you. You are my rock and my salvation. When doubt attempts to creep into my mind, you anchor me. When I struggle in life, I know you will carry me through. I know that if I trust you, nothing difficult can knock me down. You raise me up and turn my weaknesses into strengths.

Father, build up my faith in you. Strengthen my faith in your Word and works. Lead me in a life of faith. Help me focus in on you in this season and all other seasons of my life. I look forward to seeing how faithfulness furthers your kingdom.

What is your anchor through the storms of life?

CSW

Not Delayed

It is not yet time for the message to come true, but that time is coming soon; the message will come true. It may seem like a long time, but be patient and wait for it, because it will surely come; it will not be delayed.

HABAKKUK 2:3 NCV

Sometimes I feel impatient, Lord. Whether it is impatience about getting a gift, being an adult, or hearing from you, I know in the deepest part of my heart and mind that your timing is perfect. Help me to never question your timing. I know I can trust you completely. I pray I bring these thoughts to the front of my mind when I feel I have been waiting forever. I know I never need to question your timing and that if I follow you closely, all good things will come at the right moment.

Father, encourage me when I feel impatient to draw near to you, I know you will listen to my concerns. I want to be patient like you. Encourage me to be patient through all times of waiting.

What encourages you in extended periods of waiting?

CSW

True Love

Love is patient, love is kind. It does not envy,
it does not boast, it is not proud.

1 CORINTHIANS 13:4 NIV

Father, thank you for true love. It's talked about in movies
and TV shows, but with you God, it's real, tangible love.
I may not be able to fully understand it, but I know your
love for me is always there. I know it is limitless and
unconditional. You made me in your image and made me
wonderfully. You know every hair on my head and every
thought in my mind. You love every part of me.

Lord, your love heals my deepest wounds, draws me in
when I'm upset, and brings me indescribable joy. It brings
me peace when I feel anxious. You love me through my
mistakes and you forgive me. Thank you for your love
that solves my problems. I pray that I would try to love
you the way you love me. Help me to love others like you
do too.

How does the abundance of God's love influence your
relationships?

CSW

Turn for Healing

"My people who are called by My name humble themselves,
and pray and seek My face, and turn from their wicked ways,
then I will hear from heaven, and I will forgive their sin
and will heal their land."

2 CHRONICLES 7:14 NASB

God, you bring restoration to the toughest situations.
I know through reading your Word that Jesus healed
many people of their disabilities and diseases. You even
brought people back to life. I ask for restoration and
healing in my life. Through prayer and praising you, I
know you will heal the darkest and deepest wounds I
experience. I know you will bring me the joy and peace I
need to heal.

Lord, remind me when I'm feeling low that I can always
turn to you. Remind me I am never alone because you
are with me. Thank you for your hope that lifts me up
when I feel down. Speak to me when I am broken and
rescue me. I know that you cover my weaknesses and
are stronger than any chaos around me. Thank you for
your healing power. Thank you for holding me close and
loving me always.

What part of your life needs the power of the restorer?

CSW

October

Even young people faint
and get exhausted;
athletic ones may stumble and fall.
But those who wait
for Yahweh's grace
will experience divine strength.

Isaiah 40:31 tpt

Set on Heaven

*Set your minds on the things that are above,
not on the things that are on earth.*
COLOSSIANS 3:2 NASB

Lord, I want my thoughts to be focused on you: on the fruit of the Spirit and on your Word. I don't want my thoughts to be filled with things of this world. Money, popularity, and clothes are worldly things I tend to think about. I pray that instead of these, you bring thoughts of you and your plan for me to mind.

Father, allow me to concentrate on these so I can carry out your plan for me. I want to serve you the best I can. I want my mind to be set on the things from above. I pray I am set on living for you. I want to further your kingdom. I pray you are the source of all my thoughts and actions. Help me to focus on the important things in life.

Do you ever stop to consider the source and the fruit of your thoughts?

CJW

Temporary

We do not look at the things which are seen, but at the things which are not seen. For the things which are seen are temporary, but the things which are not seen are eternal.

2 CORINTHIANS 4:18 NKJV

Lord, thank you that you see everything. You see what is unseen by others. You see the time I spend in prayer or worship when no one is around. You see the hard times when I cry in my room or feel really upset. You see it all. I know you are watching over me and I am never alone. Thank you that you're always with me. You see me, have a plan for me, and your timing is perfect.

Lord, I pray that I am steadfast on you and your plan for me. Encourage me to follow you closely and be humble, as serving you often goes unseen. Remind me that things of this earth are only temporary, so focusing on you is the best thing I can do to follow you. Thank you that I will be able to spend eternity with you.

What has been occupying your thoughts lately?

CJW

Empathy

If one part suffers, every part suffers with it;
if one part is honored, every part rejoices with it.
1 CORINTHIANS 12:26 NIV

Father, I know you care for me more than I can understand. You love me completely. Help me to love you back in a similar way. You feel the hurt I feel just like you experience the joy I feel. You went before me and dealt with pain so that I could be victorious through you. Thank you that you go through my life with me and that I am never truly alone.

Not only are you kind, Father, but you are empathetic. Teach me to be empathetic toward others in the way you are. Encourage me to show care and compassion to those around me. I know if I show people compassion, they may draw nearer to you. I know it will help heal them. Thank you that something as small as a smile could brighten someone's day. Encourage me to be a hopeful light in the dark for others.

What has empathy shown you about the character of Christ?

CSW

Joy Is Medicine

A joyful, cheerful heart brings healing to both body and soul.
But the one whose heart is crushed
struggles with sickness and depression.

PROVERBS 17:22 TPT

Father, your joy in incredible. In the darkest places, your joy brings light and life. It transforms the most challenging days into good ones, and it heals all heartbreak. Your joy is incomparable to anything on earth. It brings smiles and laughter to those who have been depressed, upset, or hopeless. It heals me too.

Lord, thank you for your joy. I pray I choose joy all the days of my life no matter how I am feeling. Pour out your joy in my life. Help me to pass your joy to others who need it. I pray I bring life, light, and love to people. Just like you do for those who follow you. I pray I lift you high and obey your guidance and steps. I want to praise you with joyfulness forever and ever.

What brings you joy?

CSW

My Name

> "See, I have written your name on my hand.
> Jerusalem, I always think about your walls."
> ISAIAH 49:16 NCV

Lord, you know me better than I know myself. You formed me in my mother's womb—every hair, every little detail. You made me perfectly in your image. You see me as your child and ensure I am taken care of and loved. I am so grateful to be part of your family. I ask that when I pray, you show me more of who I am and who I should become. Teach me to walk in godly ways.

Father, when I feel doubtful about myself or my looks, I pray you silence those negative thoughts. Remind me of who I am to you and how you see me. Remind me that I am your child, worthy of all love, forgiveness, and redemption. Help me to be positive about myself and who I am. Thank you for loving me. You are such a good father.

How does knowing that the Father loves you affect your thoughts about yourself?

Get It Right

"Where your treasure is,
there will your heart be also."
LUKE 12:34 ESV

Father, I see you in the little things. The raindrops on flower petals, rainbows in the sky after a storm, and the different sunsets you paint in the sky. Thank you for such beauty. I treasure your creation. I treasure the people I care about too. Thank you for placing me in the life that I have. I am so grateful for all my friends and family. I pray that they know you and live for you like I want to.

God, help me focus on treasures you find vital so that my heart is pure and full of you. I treasure these things, but most importantly, I treasure you. Encourage me to pray to you often and draw closer to you through your Word. Help me put you first in my heart and mind. I love you, God.

What does your heart treasure?

CSW

Not Worried

Anxiety weighs down the human heart,
but a good word cheers it up.
PROVERBS 12:25 NRSV

Worrying about life comes too easily to my mind, Jesus. I know that anxieties like to creep into my thoughts. I pray against any fears and anxieties in my life; they are not of you and do not have a place in my mind. If you are with me, what can overwhelm me? Nothing can. Your name is stronger than any of my worries, Prince of Peace. I know that you will bring healing and peace that surpasses all understanding. Thank you that even though you know everything, you listen to me with compassion.

Lord, I belong in your presence, protected by you. I may feel surrounded, but I know that I am surrounded by you. I know with you I am safe and secure. Turn my worries into joy that can only come from you. Thank you that in your presence, I am at perfect peace.

How does God's Word offer peace to your heart and encourage you?

CBW

Wealth of Character

Choose a good reputation over great riches;
being held in high esteem is better than silver or gold.
PROVERBS 22:1 NLT

Father, I know money does not equal happiness. It does not bring joy or meaning to life. I pray I always remember that. Important possessions in life are not riches of this world. They are riches from you and of you. The valuable possessions of this world are the fruit of the Spirit. Those are love, joy, peace, patience, kindness, goodness, faithfulness, gentleness, and self-control.

God, if I am rich in these, my reputation will be honorable, and I will grow close to you. I will be able to love others the way you do and live my life to its fullest. By focusing on these, I will be a light in the dark and follow you closely all the days of my life. Encourage me to draw near to you and learn more about who you are. Help me to study your Word and what it means to be fruitful.

What fruit of the Spirit can you act on today?

Call to Love

Do not rejoice when your enemy falls,
And do not let your heart be glad when he stumbles.
PROVERBS 24:17 NKJV

God, it may seem easy to feel people get what they deserve sometimes. Help me to not allow those thoughts into my mind. I know a reaction like that is not one you have. I want to be like you in everything I do. Please help me to leave vengeance to you as your Word says. Instead of believing someone got what they deserved, allow me to act humbly and pray for that person to get to know you.

Help my thoughts to always be about expanding your kingdom and furthering your plans. Thank you, Lord, that you are merciful and caring. Thank you that you forgive me always. I know you love me even when I make mistakes, I'm so grateful for your compassion. Help me to forgive those who have hurt me. I want to love my enemies, as hard as that can be!

How do you react when those you find difficult seem to get what's due them?

Strength Revealed

Yours, LORD, is the greatness and the power
and the glory and the majesty and the splendor,
for everything in heaven and earth is yours.
1 CHRONICLES 29:11 NIV

Lord, thank you that you are strong. You cover all my weaknesses and build me up in my weaknesses to make me strong. You work through me to raise me up in you and your plan for me. I'm so glad you have a plan for my life and that all I need to do is follow you. Help me to obey you, even when it may seem hard.

Lord, you are not only strong, but powerful too. Through you, I know I can accomplish anything—even miracles. I pray you use me to heal those around me. I pray you encourage me to share your heart with those who don't know you. I know if I draw near to you, you will make my path and decisions clear. Thank you for the work you've already done in my life and the work you will do through me.

Where can you see God's power at work in your life?

CSW

The Only Judge

God is the only Lawmaker and Judge.
He is the only One who can save and destroy.
So it is not right for you to judge your neighbor.
JAMES 4:12 NCV

Judgment can be easy to pass on others, God. Taking one look at someone and deciding what I think about them happens quickly. Judgment should only be given by you; help me to leave it to you. In your Word it says that you will have vengeance, so I do not need to worry about it. Thank you for taking care of me. When I feel myself passing judgment, remind me it is not my place.

God, encourage me to remember the significance of forgiveness. Teach me to forgive those who persecute me. I am so thankful for your forgiveness that cleanses all sin and wipes all pain away. Thank you that mercy trumps judgment and that you are a merciful God. I know I can trust you. Thank you for being gracious and affectionate.

Do you trust that God can judge more rightly than you can?

Faithful in Little

"The one who is faithful in a very little thing is also faithful in much; and the one who is unrighteous in a very little thing is also unrighteous in much."

LUKE 16:10 NASB

God, I pray that I will be faithful in the little things so that I can be faithful in the more important ones too. Help me to enjoy the small things in life like the flowers on the side of the road, or people that pass me and smile or say hi. Encourage me to draw near to you and pray about the little things like when I get upset over something trivial or want help completing a small task.

Father, help me to come to you always. I know if I am faithful in little things, I am also faithful in much. Help me not to write "little sins" like white lies off as unimportant, but rather understand that sin is all the same in your eyes and it keeps me from growing closer to you. I want to be more like you. Encourage me to thank you for the little things.

What areas of your life have you been writing off as unimportant?

CSW

Honest Worship

Oh come, let us worship and bow down;
let us kneel before the LORD, our Maker!

PSALM 95:6 ESV

Father, I love worshipping you. I sing songs about your greatness or how beautiful you are because I want you to see how much I love you. Worship also gives me a sense of community. Usually, worship happens during a church service where I am surrounded by my brothers and sisters in Christ who love you like I do. Thank you for the community I am in. Worshipping you together is a beautiful thing.

Lord, help me to praise you always. To show you how much I appreciate you through songs and prayers. Encourage me to mediate on your Word or sing my own songs to you in quiet moments alone. Help me to feel the presence of your Holy Spirit. Draw me near to you in these times and keep me close. Thank you for the joy, peace, and love I feel when I spend time with you. It is truly a blessing to praise you.

What can you praise God for right now?

CSW

Wonderfully Made

I praise you, for I am fearfully and wonderfully made.
Wonderful are your works; that I know very well.

PSALM 139:14 NRSV

Lord, you are the Creator. Your creation is beautifully and wonderfully made. Thank you that you made me. I am so grateful for the beauty I see in the world every day. Whether it's a meadow full of flowers, a waterfall, or the starry sky at night. Thank you for the sky; every day it looks different but has its own beautiful characteristics. I am blessed to be surrounded by such incredible creation.

God, you made me in your image; I thank you for that. You made me unique and that shows me how much you love me. You did not choose to create me to look the same as everyone else. Each person is special; you spent your time creating everything from every hair on my head to the color of my eyes to the way my toes look. Every detail is unique. Thank you for making me wonderfully. Thank you that I am your child.

Where do you see the reflection of God's beauty today?

CEW

Qualified

It is not that we think we are qualified to do anything on our own.
Our qualification comes from God.
2 Corinthians 3:5 nlt

Father, thank you for your grace that covers all sin and weaknesses. You forgive me and give me a clean slate. I'm so grateful for your grace. Where I feel weak, I know you make me strong. I pray in areas of weakness for me, whether envy, deceit, or anger, you would work on those areas in my life.

God, turn my envy into gratitude for what I have. Turn any deceit into truth and honor. Turn my anger into joy and grace for others. Encourage me to be more like you in all aspects of my life. I know that without you, I would get nowhere. I pray you remind me that my qualification comes from you and only you. I need you. I know that with you, nothing is impossible.

Are you confident that God's grace covers all your weaknesses?

CSW

Meant for Good

You intended to harm me, but God intended it for good to accomplish what is now being done, the saving of many lives.
GENESIS 50:20 NKJV

God, sometimes people in my life hurt me. During those times, help me to remember that you love me unconditionally and I am never alone. Thank you that you heal and restore me no matter how deep the wounds feel. Thank you that bad situations often turn into positive life lessons. I find they also make me stronger in my faith.

Lord, sometimes the pain I've felt has pushed me closer to you and made me more confident in who I am—a child of the King of kings. I pray I grow closer to you whenever I face challenges. You are the redeemer. You turn disaster into personal growth. I want to remember your incomparable strength when I feel weak. Thank you that you are a good father.

How have you seen God's redemption in terrible situations?

CAW

Confident Faith

Faith is confidence in what we hope for
and assurance about what we do not see.
HEBREWS 11:1 NIV

God, there are so many things that I desire for my future.
You know the longings of my heart and I am reassured
when I read your Word that your plan is better than mine.
By believing you have a purpose for me, I can rest in
peace each day no matter what trials afflict me.

Thank you for your guidance and steadfast love, Jesus.
Because you died and rose again for me I have no fear of
the future. It is your will that my strength comes from you
and you alone.

What builds your confidence in God?

AF

Genuine Love

Let love be genuine. Abhor what is evil;
hold fast to what is good.
ROMANS 12:9 ESV

God, the world surrounding me is filled with evil and temptations, but I know that if I keep my faith grounded in your Word, evil has no power over me. When I struggle to do what is right, fill me with your love because your love is a light in a world of darkness. With your love surrounding me, I am safe and reassured. Only through your love can I walk on the path of righteousness, turning away from sin, and continuing on the path you have destined for me.

Father, each day teach me how to show others your genuine love so they too may turn away from sin and embrace a life filled with hope and joy. I don't want to give to others in hopes of receiving praise or something in return. Instead, let every gift I give be fully from you and done in secret because things given in secret are seen and blessed by you.

Are you loving out of an abundance of the love God gives, or giving it away hoping you'll receive something in return?

Willing to Listen

A wise warning to someone who will listen
is as valuable as gold earrings or fine gold jewelry.
PROVERBS 25:12 NCV

God, there are things that I desire that are not a part of your plan. Sometimes I stumble and fall into sin. When things avert me from your path, teach me to listen to wise counsel whether that be from my parents, friends, or a mentor. Open my eyes to see the fault in my ways, not so that I may be ashamed, but so I can ask for your forgiveness and learn from my mistakes.

Father, when my mind wants to rebel, teach my heart how to stand firm in my faith so I do not stray from the abundant life you have promised me. Whenever I receive counsel from others, help me to set pride aside and hear the words of wisdom they have to offer.

Are you willing to listen to a wise friend's warning?

AF

Better than Life

Because Your favor is better than life,
My lips will praise You.
PSALM 63:3 NASB

God, you have blessed me with such an amazing life. Even when trials arise, with you beside me nothing can bring me down. Your love and joy surround me! Thank you for every blessing you put in my life and have planned for my future.

Jesus, I know that because you made the ultimate sacrifice for me by dying on the cross, death has no power over me and I never have to fear anything in this world. This life cannot compare to the life you have ready for me in eternity which is better than anything I can imagine. Through my everyday tasks, I will sing praises to you because you have delivered me from my sin. You bless me in ways that I cannot fathom, for only you know what my future holds and how trials now will lead to blessings later.

How has God's love surprised you?

Without Regret

Godly grief produces a repentance that leads to salvation and brings no regret, but worldly grief produces death.
2 CORINTHIANS 7:10 NRSV

God, Sometimes I am ashamed when my faith is weak. I begin to worry that my faith will not carry me through hardships in my life. Will I still believe and declare your name when I am put to the test? There have been times when I turn away from an opportunity to share your Word with another because I am afraid I will be rejected.

Jesus, I know that regret from past sins is not here to bring me down, but instead to turn me in the right direction. Whenever I feel ashamed of my sin, I remember that you washed me white as snow by atoning for my sin through your death on the cross.

How has forgiveness shaped the way you deal with pain in your life?

AF

No More Boulders

*"Build up, build up, prepare the road!
Remove the obstacles out of the way of my people."*
ISAIAH 57:14 NIV

God, there are stumbling blocks around every corner.
School, social pressure, worry about the future—these
are just a few things that are pulling me down. When my
faith is weak and I let these things control me, give me
the strength to look past the present struggles.

Father, I will take on the problems at hand with joy and
confidence because you give me everything I need to
succeed. No trouble is greater than you, so what shall I
fear? The Creator of the world is on my side!

What obstacles have kept you stuck in one place
for too long?

AF

Pursuing Peace

*Let us pursue the things which make for peace
and the things by which one may edify another.*
ROMANS 14:19 NKJV

God, you know the desires of my heart. There are so
many things I want to do and places I want to go. When
I compare the few things I have accomplished in my life
with the things I want to do, I get anxious. My heart is
being pulled in so many directions and I feel like I can't
give my all to anything.

Lord, I know that your way is better than my way. Teach
me to pursue you first before anything else because only
through pursuing you are the other things worthwhile.

What has your heart been pursuing?

AF

Come to Me

"Come to me, all who labor and are heavy laden,
and I will give you rest."
MATTHEW 11:28 ESV

God, sometimes I feel like every second of my day is taken up and I have no time to accomplish all that I need to do. When night comes, I am drained and dejected. In these moments, I will turn to you. I try to go through the day relying on my own strength believing that I can do things on my own. I am so wrong!

Father, without you helping me, tasks have no meaning and my strength fails me. You bring purpose to everything I do, so I will go to you not only when I am weak and distraught but always. Anyone can reach out to you when times are hard but it's when things are easy that I must turn to you also. Not in my strength alone but through your strength can I do all things.

When the weight of life is too much, where do you turn?

AF.

Approaching the End

Since we are approaching the end of all things, be intentional, purposeful, and self-controlled so that you can be given to prayer.
1 PETER 4:7 TPT

God, when I read your Word I am inspired by those who worked endlessly not for worldly success but for your glory. I know that my time on this earth is limited and one day I will join you in eternity.

Father, with the days I have left, I want to serve others and work for your goodwill. I don't want to please myself or be accomplished by earthly standards but make a way for others to find you. Distractions surround me, calling for my attention, but I choose to seek you first.

How does self-discipline make space in your life?

AF

Sharpened by Iron

As iron sharpens iron,
so a friend sharpens a friend.
PROVERBS 27:17 NLT

God, a good and faithful friend keeps me accountable and inspires me to keep pursuing you. Not only do I want to be supported by my brothers and sisters in Christ, but I also want to support them. When they become disheartened or stray from your way, give me the wisdom to help them.

Father, work through me to be a good example to my friends. Reveal spiritual mentors you have placed in my life or are going to place in my life. Just like Jesus surrounded himself with the disciples, I want to surround myself with godly, faithful friends who will encourage me to pursue you.

Who keeps you accountable?

AF

Walk on Water

He said, "Come." And when Peter had come down out of the boat, he walked on the water to go to Jesus.
MATTHEW 14:29 NKJV

God, you know the hopes I have for my future. All the things I want to do with my life seem important to me now, but you see the bigger picture. You know my life and the plans you have for me are greater than anything I could imagine. I walk to you when you call me because I trust your love.

Lord, nothing can happen in my life that can't work for your glory. Trials will arise and my faith will be tested, but over and over again you call me back to your love. Broken are the chains that were holding me down because I am freed from every burden, anxiety, sadness, and sin. I choose to set down these broken chains and walk to you.

What is holding you back from stepping out where God is calling you?

AF

No Despair

The righteous person may have many troubles,
but the LORD delivers him from them all.

PSALM 34:19 NIV

God, for all my days on this earth I will be surrounded by evil: peer pressure, lust, anxiety, hatred, and much more. When I lose my way and follow a path of sin, I feel defeated. But you are greater than every evil in this world. The same God who overcame death on the cross delivers me from my troubles.

Jesus, deliver me from talking back to my parents, gossiping about others, getting angry with my siblings, and letting things of this world distract me from you. Trials will always arise, but when they do I will turn to you for strength and guidance.

What trouble do you need deliverance from?

AF

Beyond Reason

What should we say about this?
If God is for us, no one can defeat us.
ROMANS 8:31 NCV

God, there is no greater sacrifice than laying down your life for another. It's one thing to die for a loved one but to die for the very people who are putting you to death is a kind of mercy and love no one could ever fathom.

Father, you speak life into everything I do. There isn't a task at hand that you aren't willing to help me with. You show me everything I need to know about living life to the fullest. All I need to do to be confident in your love is open my heart to your teachings which are found in your living Word.

Do you believe that God is for you?

AF

Surrendered

Instead, you ought to say,
"If the Lord wills, we will live and also do this or that."
JAMES 4:15 NCV

God, my life is your life. I have no life aside from the one you gave me. If I choose to follow my own path, I know that will lead down the road of destruction. Every time I fight against your will or believe I can do things on my own, I fall flat on my face. My legs cannot move in the right direction without your guidance.

Jesus, if life is meaningless and frugal without you, why would I ever try to go against your will? You have greater plans than my plans because you can see all of eternity where I can only imagine what the next few weeks, months, and years could be. Nothing I do is certain but your will and love. Help me to embrace them.

If God were to change the direction of your future, how would you react?

AF

More Grace

He gives more grace. Therefore it says,
"God opposes the proud, but gives grace to the humble."
JAMES 4:6 ESV

God, in a world that teaches being the best requires climbing the social ladder, it's hard to remain humble when the opportunity for evil arises. I could so easily chase the dream of success and build my self-worth through gaining a higher status. But at the end of my life, what will that bring me? I will have nothing when I die except your love. So, I give my all to you.

Jesus, you were the best example of living a humble life. You washed the feet of your disciples and spoke to those who were hated by other people. If you could do that, I should be able to obey my parents, serve my friends, and give abundantly to those around me. The more I work toward living like you did, the better my life will be.

What do you need more of from the Lord today?

AF

November

Pay close attention, my child,
to your father's wise words
and never forget your mother's instructions.
For their insight will bring you success,
adorning you with grace-filled thoughts
and giving you reins
to guide your decisions.

PROVERBS 1:8-9 TPT

Rest in Safety

"You will have confidence, because there is hope;
you will be protected and take your rest in safety."
JOB 11:18 NRSV

God, people are constantly pulling other people down.
Girls gossip about their supposed friends. Guys tease
the non-athletic kid. Parents shame the rebellious teen.
Teachers give up on struggling students. How can I have
hope when I am surrounded by people who only see the
worst?

God, help me not to have a mask of depression around
my eyes because that is not what you see. There is
nothing in this world that can bring me down. When
my faith is weak and worries surround me, I pray for
a hopeful mindset—one that sees the big picture of
eternity. No defeat in this life will carry into heaven.

When your hope is dwindling, where do you turn for
encouragement?

AF

Pray for Others

Confess your sins to each other and pray for each other so that you may be healed. The earnest prayer of a righteous person has great power and produces wonderful results.

JAMES 5:16 NLT

God, a huge way I communicate with you is through prayer. In every situation, I can pray. I should be praying more often instead of trying to fix the problem on my own first. When I pray for others, I sometimes feel like my prayers aren't being heard or they hold no value. What will happen when I bring my friend's struggles to you through prayer? Will they be heard?

Father, you say pray for those who are mean to you, so praying for a friend is surely valued as well. Today I pray for my friends who are hurting and in need of your love. They feel something is missing and there is no one supporting them. Please reassure them that you are right there with them.

When was the last time you prayed with a friend?

AF

Voice of Prayer

Certainly God has heard me;
He has attended to the voice of my prayer.

PSALM 66:19 NKJV

God, many times when I pray I feel like I am not being heard. I can't always see the results that I want or when I want. But I know that what I pray for is heard and if you don't answer in the way I want, it's not because you are ignoring me. Rather, I need to be patient and watch for the way you work.

Father, if I pray for a youth group where I can grow in my faith, but none ever present themselves as good options, does that mean you didn't hear my prayer? No, it simply means it is not in your timing for me. Maybe instead you want me to seek you on my own so I can build my relationship with you before getting caught up in other things. You hear every prayer from me and answer in your own timing.

When was the last time God answered one of your prayers?

AF

Not Alone

The LORD God said, "It is not good for the man to be alone.
I will make a helper suitable for him."
GENESIS 2:18 NIV

God, I don't like it when people tell me what to do. I think I know what's best and want to feel accomplished by doing things on my own. When I rely on people, they can let me down. But do blessings come from trusting others to support me? You want people to live in the community and help one another.

Father, from bad experiences of trusting others, I have been cautious to confide in people. Soften my heart, so I see them through your eyes. When I understand that people make mistakes even when they have good intentions, I will be more willing to share my burdens with others. A good friendship is a blessing from you.

Do you depend on yourself more than others?

Golden Rule

"Do to others what you want them to do to you. This is the
meaning of the law of Moses and the teaching of the prophets."
MATTHEW 7:12 NCV

God, I want to have a servant's heart, just like Jesus did.
To many, serving is something they do to get things in
return. I clean my room so I can go to my friend's house,
I go to work only to get money, or I help pass out papers
in class to make the teacher like me. Many things I do
that seem like they are coming from a servant's heart are
really coming from greed and selfish pursuits.

Father, you say to give in secret and expect nothing in
return. When I give in secret, I am filled with a joy that I
can't explain. You bless me in greater ways when I serve
like Jesus than when I serve for my own benefit. I will
take each day as an opportunity to love, serve, and listen
to others in the same way you ask others to do to me.

Are your attitudes and actions consistent with how you
expect to be treated by others?

AF

Let Love Rule

In addition to all these things put on love,
which is the perfect bond of unity.

COLOSSIANS 3:14 NASB

God, keeping my feelings hidden is a way that I protect myself from being hurt. But if no one knows how I feel, that means they also haven't experienced my kindness or love. In order to fully love others the way you love me, I need to let down my walls and trust in you as my only defense.

Father, I don't need to be hidden and afraid to show my feelings to others. With your love, any person's rejection can't hurt me. I am confident in who I am and no one can change the way you see me. When I begin to love others generously, I build stronger relationships. Teach me to accept rejection from others and keep loving them in spite of it. No walls can be broken by being passive in my emotions or relationships.

How freely does love flow from your life?

AF.

Always Calling

"I have not come to call the righteous
but sinners to repentance."
LUKE 5:32 ESV

God, being with you is never boring. I used to think if
I gave my life to Jesus, I would miss out on fun. But is
having no purpose fun? I have a purpose when I follow
you. I have a reason to wake up and it brings joy into the
dullest of situations.

Father, what I love about having faith is it will never
stop growing. You test me and mature me, constantly
revealing new wonders that I couldn't have imagined.
Thank you for continuing to lead me in every moment.
When I lose track of your plan, show me how to submit
again. Each day I wake up and submit my worries, fear,
troubles, and every thought to you.

How does it make you feel when you consider God is
writing your story as you submit to him?

AF

Greater Good

We know love by this, that he laid down his life for us—
and we ought to lay down our lives for one another.
1 JOHN 3:16 NRSV

God, my first instant isn't to serve others around me. My top priorities are often self-focused. But this isn't how Jesus lived. I want to lay down my selfish desires and love like Jesus loved. He died for me, so surely I can learn to be a servant to those around me.

In every situation today, Father, show me how to look for ways to help others. Even when people don't ask for help or are rude to me, I will choose to be humble and continue to serve and love them. I know that loving in the face of adversity will be tough for me alone, so I pray for strength and guidance as I go through this day.

How can you choose love today?

AF

What If

"Don't be concerned about what to eat and what to drink.
Don't worry about such things."
LUKE 12:29 NLT

God, worry only distracts me from what matters. I know that all worry is overcome by you because you promise me constant peace. I never have to stress about money, school, or relationships. All I have to do is believe that you have more power than my problems.

In moments when my worry is overwhelming and I don't know where to turn, I choose to turn to you, Lord. The people you love will never be forgotten. When I feel like you aren't there and worry is closing in, I will trust you and rest in your peace. Any anxiety or stress is only a tool the enemy uses to cripple my faith. If I continue to have faith in you, those feelings will never have any power over me.

What worries can you hand over to God today?

Hold on Tight

Remember to stay alert and hold firmly to all that you believe.
Be mighty and full of courage.

1 CORINTHIANS 16:13 TPT

God, I belong to something greater than myself. There is an eternity after I die and that eternity is ruled by a loving God. Why should I ever waste my time pursuing anything that doesn't benefit me for eternity. When I do anything, I want to do it for you. I want to show you that I love you because you have forgiven me of all my sins.

Lord, I get angry and yell. I feel stressed and overwhelmed. I let people down and walk right into sin. But even through all of this, I am loved and cherished by you. If you choose to love me, broken and all, then I can be faithful when tested. As I am continuing to develop my faith, I will mess up, but knowing that I can come back to you and still be loved makes the journey worth it.

What belief about God keeps you going when you would have given up?

AF

Life of Blessings

"Because of your father's God, who helps you,
because of the Almighty, who blesses you
with blessings of the skies above, blessings of the deep
springs below, blessings of the breast and womb."
GENESIS 49:25 NIV

God, all around me are blessings from you. I often lose sight of what you have given me because I am so focused on what I am missing. I compare my circumstances to others and think that if I had what they have, I would be fulfilled. But you say that all I need is your love to be fulfilled and joyful.

During this day, Lord, I will thank you at every opportunity for the blessings in my life. Help me to hold close your love and not the things of this world. My possessions and popularity don't go with me when I enter heaven; only your love and gifts of the Spirit do.

What blessings are you enjoying because of choices that previous generations made?

You Remain

Jesus Christ is the same
yesterday and today, and forever.
HEBREWS 13:8 NASB

God, my emotions are like a roller coaster with highs and lows. One moment I am happy and content and the next I am depressed and seeking satisfaction. You are constant and you want me to be constant in the same way. You didn't make me live life like riding a roller coaster.

Lord, I have yet to fully understand how in all moments I can be content and joyful, so I pray you would show me how I can be like this all the time. You are the foundation of my faith. In the same way you remain constant, I want to remain constant: consistently joyful, faithful, loving, and at peace. I never want to rely on anything but you.

How does God's constancy fuel your faith?

AF

Wisdom from God

When the people of Israel heard about King Solomon's decision, they respected him very much. They saw he had wisdom from God to make the right decisions.

1 KINGS 3:28 NCV

God, I feel like I have so many choices, with each one leading to a major change in my life. Where am I going to college? Who should I be friends with? Where should I get a job? What should I major in? I have so many decisions I need to make, but I don't know what to choose.

When I feel overwhelmed and confused, I ask that you would give me peace, Father. You already know my future, and no matter what decision I make, it will work for your good. In every situation, I pray for guidance to choose what would most glorify you.

How do you make major decisions in your life?

Out of Hiding

Whoever conceals his transgressions will not prosper,
but he who confesses and forsakes them will obtain mercy.
PROVERBS 28:13 ESV

God, sometimes I think that if I hide the bad parts of who I am, it will make me a better person. They are still there but I think if I don't acknowledge what I've done wrong, then I can pretend that it's not there. I don't need to hide anything from you because you already know me better than anyone could ever know me. You created me so how could I ever hide myself from you?

Father, what amazes me each day is how beautiful you think I am. If the world says my looks or personality is lacking, it doesn't matter because I was made perfectly by you. I will not hide from you; instead, I come to you when I'm troubled or joyful because you love me either way.

What is keeping you from coming to the Lord with all that you are?

AF

Mercy Undeserved

I was given mercy so that in me, the worst of all sinners, Christ Jesus could show that he has patience without limit. His patience with me made me an example for those who would believe in him and have life forever.

1 TIMOTHY 1:16 NCV

God, your mercy is like nothing I could ever comprehend. Even trying to compare it to the mercy I know on earth doesn't make sense because what you did for me is like nothing anyone has ever done for another person. Sacrificing your life for a loved one is a noble act in itself but going through torture brought upon by your own people and dying while praying for the people who hate you is beyond imaginable. That is a mercy that passes my understanding.

Father, I know there is power in a love like that. When I rebel against my parents, talk badly about other people, yell at my siblings, or disobey a teacher, I know that you look past those things. You are in my corner, rooting for my success. You see me fall, but you also help me get right back up. I hope I never forget your mercy because it is such a wonderful, never-ending gift.

What do you think of God's mercy?

AF

Celebrate Perfection

"Why do you call me good?" Jesus asked.
"Only God is truly good."
MARK 10:18 NLT

God, I have so many faults and holes in who I am. You promise to come in and fill those holes and give me purpose. I will always be a mixture of good and bad because I am human, but I know that as long as I have faith in you, I will always be fulfilled and whole.

Lord, by allowing you to work in my life I open the door to the endless blessings you promise me. Thank you for giving me such a wonderful life. When things get hard, I will lean on your goodness and love.

How does God's goodness fill your life?

Friend of God

One who has unreliable friends soon comes to ruin,
but there is a friend who sticks closer than a brother.

PROVERBS 18:24 NIV

God, there is no relationship that is more important than the one I have with you. Other people will let me down in the same way I have let my own friends down. No one can ever love me as fully as you love me because you know me better than anyone else. When I get caught up in the difficulties of relationships, I will rely on my friendship with you because you never fail me.

Sometimes I feel like even the people who are closest to me don't fully know me. But you know me. You created me and you want to show me who I am and why I am so loved by you. My confidence rests in you, Lord, for you are the rock that I can rest on.

Do you trust God's friendship to stick with you through thick and thin?

AF

Thank You

Let us be thankful, because we have a kingdom that cannot be shaken. We should worship God in a way that pleases him with respect and fear.

HEBREWS 12:28 NCV

God, I look at what other people have. I think that I don't have enough. I need more clothes, money, popularity, and travel pictures. But what will I get from those things? Even if I had all the money in the world, I would not be fulfilled.

Being a part of your kingdom is worth more than any expensive clothes or beach trip, Lord. I am promised a life in heaven where gifts will be abundant. I choose to be content with what I have because all I need is faith in you to be richer than kings.

What about God's kingdom are you thankful for?

AF

Prayer of Faith

The prayer of faith will save the sick,
and the Lord will raise him up.
And if he has committed sins,
he will be forgiven.

JAMES 5:15 NKJV

God, the future can often feel like a dark place. It is unknown and could hold many difficulties. I remember that your goodness is greater than anything that could happen.

Father, when I am anxious about the future, I will remember all the good things you have done in my life and hold onto those. They will get me through any trial because they hold the promise of good things to come. Thank you for forgiving me of my sins so I can experience your goodness.

When you consider God's goodness at work in your life, how does that make you think about the future?

AF

Constant Praise

Let every activity of your lives and every word that comes from your lips be drenched with the beauty of our Lord Jesus, the Anointed One. And bring your constant praise to God the Father because of what Christ has done for you!

COLOSSIANS 3:17 TPT

God, my hidden actions and thoughts are seen by you. What better way to glorify your name than by following your will even when it seems no one is watching. I honor you with my thoughts because my thoughts matter. I praise you with my actions because they show how much I love you. Each time I choose to follow your Word, I am giving thanks to you.

Father, when I could be watching TV or scrolling through social media, I will use that time to read my Bible and pray. Speaking deceit, hate, or gossip while praising you from the same mouth is not honoring you. I thank you for your goodness to me by praising you with my whole heart: in every word, action, and thought.

How can you thank God for his goodness today?

No Better Gift

The Spirit of the LORD will rest on Him,
The spirit of wisdom and understanding,
The spirit of counsel and strength,
The spirit of knowledge and the fear of the LORD.

ISAIAH 11:2 NASB

God, the greatest gift of all is the promise of eternal life with you. Through this promise, I can live each day as you want me to live. I pray for wisdom in every situation to guide my choices and help those around me. Give me people in my life who will support me in my faith and encourage me to press into your Word. Help me use your Word like a guide and a weapon against evil.

Father, if I am equipped with the knowledge you gave me through the Bible, I can overcome any fear. Each day is a new beginning because you renew me and give me a chance to change. I don't have to be depressed when I feel alone because you are always there for me. There is no better gift than my faith in you.

How does walking with the Spirit enrich your life?

AF

In Kindness

*"You gave me life and showed me kindness,
and in your providence watched over my spirit."*
JOB 10:12 NIV

God, you tell me to always be kind to others even the people who hurt me. Why should I be kind to people who hurt me? Wouldn't I be justified in being mean back? You say that there is a better kind of justice. If someone hurts me and I am kind back to them they won't know how to react. They will wonder what I have that makes me so kind and joyful.

Lord, this is why I should always be kind because kind people attract non-believers. When someone pays for my food in the drive-through or offers to help me when I am struggling, I feel your love working through them. Thank you for your kindness. Help me to show others this type of love as well.

How does kindness change your perception of someone?

True Humility

He poured water into the basin, and began washing the disciples' feet and wiping them with the towel which He had tied around Himself.
JOHN 13:5 NASB

God, I am usually caught up in my own troubles and plans. I am not thinking about how to help those around me but on how I can make myself feel happy, accomplished, or satisfied. When I only do things for myself I don't feel that way for long. Joy is fleeting when I am only looking out for myself.

Lord, when I choose to clean for someone without being asked, pick up food for a friend, or sacrifice my time for another person, I feel more happy, accomplished, and satisfied than if I were to just serve myself. I don't want to serve only to make myself feel like a good person; I want to serve from a humble heart expecting nothing in return.

How can you humbly serve someone today?

AF

Approach Boldly

Let us therefore approach the throne of grace with boldness, so that we may receive mercy and find grace to help in time of need.

HEBREWS 4:16 NRSV

God, there is no mercy greater than the mercy you demonstrated on the cross. You forgive me each time I make a mistake even when I make the same mistake multiple times. When I go against your will, I approach you in humility and ask you to forgive me once again. If you can forgive me of all my sins, I can show mercy to those who have hurt me.

Father, soften my heart to those I hold grudges against. Break down the walls guarding my heart and teach me to love instead of reject and hate. Being bold means being different and not many people are quick to forgive. Show me this kind of boldness, so I can walk in forgiveness when my selfish side would rather hold a grudge.

Do you have mercy to give to others?

AF.

A Clean Heart

Create in me a clean heart, O God,
and put a new and right spirit within me.
PSALM 51:10 NRSV

God, I am drawn to things that don't please you. It's easier to lie, steal, cheat, gossip, and do countless other evil acts than to choose the life you plan for me. At least, it's easier to do those things when I don't have you by my side. When I remember that you are with me always, watching and guiding me, then it becomes easier to choose to walk in the right Spirit. It's like turning my GPS on mute. If I can't hear the directions, I don't know which way to go.

Lord, in the same way, I need to turn on my ears to listen for your words of wisdom so when I am at a crossroads between sin and holiness, I choose holiness. Today, I turn on my spiritual GPS so you can bring renewal in my life.

What needs the renewing touch of the Spirit in your life?

AF

Fueled Belief

"Will you never believe in me
unless you see miraculous signs and wonders?"
JOHN 4:48 NLT

God, for many, seeing is believing. You say to walk by faith because faith is not seeing but believing despite not having tangible evidence before me. The only thing I need to believe in you is faith: faith that you are God and faith that everything written in your Word is truth.

I want to dive deeper into your Word, Father, because there I find my heart is strengthened. When I read my Bible, I know you are planting seeds for future growth. I will continue to read your Word and pray so I don't lose my belief because nothing is more important to me than my faith.

What fuels your belief in God?

Way to Peace

All this is from God. Through Christ, God made peace between us and himself, and God gave us the work of telling everyone the peace we can have with him.

2 CORINTHIANS 5:18 NCV

God, I often try to fix my problems on my own. I don't want to rely on someone to help me for fear that they will let me down. I don't know if I can fully confide in my friends because they might judge me or not care about what I am saying.

Who can I turn to when I feel like I have no one to support me? I know you say you're always there for me, but sometimes I feel alone. When I feel alone and in need of peace, I turn to you, God. You are there for me in every situation ready to support and guide me through the worst.

Do you confidently believe that you can go to God with anything at any time?

AF

Not Feeling It

Diligent hands will rule,
but laziness ends in forced labor.
PROVERBS 12:24 NIV

God, forced labor is something everyone will have to endure at some point in their life. I am forced to do the dishes. I am forced to go to school. I can choose to do this labor diligently or I could choose to walk through the task with a lazy attitude. You say that laziness ends in forced labor. I will never excel in your blessing if I don't apply myself at each opportunity.

Father, I am motivated because I know that if I put my all into everything I do, I will be glorifying you through my actions. You say a heart that glorifies you is blessed abundantly. Therefore, I will be blessed not limited to worldly blessings but also in my relationships, my heart, and my soul.

What is your motivation for work?

Wait for Promises

You need to persevere so that when you have done
the will of God, you will receive what he has promised.
HEBREWS 10:36 NIV

God, your will is for me to persevere through every trial.
Being a Christian comes with difficulties because the
world is filled with evil, but those difficulties have no
power over me. How can I run away from trials when you
say that blessings are waiting for me on the other side?

God, give me strength so I can continue to persevere
through hard situations and receive your blessings.
People with the strongest faith still endure hard situations
and it is not their strength that carries them through
the trials but their faith. Give me faith that can carry me
through every trial.

When hard situations arise, do you persevere
or run away?

AF

First and True

Don't set the affections of your heart on this world or in loving the things of the world. The love of the Father and the love of the world are incompatible.

1 JOHN 2:15 TPT

God, through the way I spend my time, I am not showing you love. I let my friends, school, sports, and events take priority over prayer and studying the Bible. Filling every second of the day is the way I think I am bringing meaning to my life, but it is all meaningless without you. I could have the most fun day planned with my closest friends, but if I don't take even five minutes with you, it won't be the same.

Lord, you make me a better, happier person, so setting time aside just for you benefits me. Next time I reach for my phone to mindlessly scroll through apps, I will instead reach for my Bible or close my eyes in prayer. Doing that will bring me so much more joy than anything else.

If you look at the way you spend your time, what are your affections set on?

December

"For I know the plans I have for you,"
declares the LORD, "plans to prosper
you and not to harm you, plans to
give you hope and a future."

JEREMIAH 29:11 NIV

Make Me Wise

Blessed is a person who finds wisdom,
And one who obtains understanding.
PROVERBS 3:13 NASB

God, you offer me constant peace and with that peace, wisdom. What should I say in this situation? Where should I go to college? How should I respond to that person? These are all questions that you can answer. I don't need to worry about being wise because all my wisdom comes from you.

Father, when I am in a dilemma and confused about which way to go, show me your will. I want to grow in understanding because by growing in understanding and wisdom, I am developing a better relationship with you. Teach me to ask for wisdom in every situation so I follow your will and receive your blessing.

What do you need wisdom about?

Ever Brighter

We all, with unveiled face, beholding as in a mirror the glory of the Lord, are being transformed into the same image from glory to glory, just as by the Spirit of the Lord.

2 CORINTHIANS 3:18 NKJV

God, you transform me into a new person when I accept you into my heart. I've heard stories of people who are completely changed by your love. Do that to me, Lord. Change me into your perfect image and fulfill my longing to be unique and whole. In my life, I want to reflect your characteristics by loving others, serving my parents and friends, applying myself at every task, and walking in all the fruit of the Spirit.

Father, develop my character when I go through hardships today, tomorrow, and for the rest of my life so they don't defeat me but make me stronger. The more I lean on you, the better I will become. I will be a better daughter, sister, and friend because I am made whole by you.

What characteristics are shining bright in your life?

AF

Striving

> "Don't work for the food that spoils. Work for the food that stays good always and gives eternal life. The Son of Man will give you this food, because on him God the Father has put his power."
>
> JOHN 6:27 NCV

God, when I reflect on what is important to me at this moment, self-image is at the top of my priority list. I am striving for success to show others what I can do and accomplish. Each day I work to earn respect from others by showing them I can lead, listen, and be independent.

Father, caring so much about approval and acceptance is so meaningless when I can find that and more in you. You offer me love that no one else can give and purpose that only I can fulfill. Why do I waste so much time and energy striving for the diminishing goal of pleasing others? From now on, I want to make you the reason I do everything. When I get ready in the morning, I look good because you say I look good. If I ace a test, I am proud because I made you proud. There isn't a task that I can do that doesn't have meaning as long as I do it for you.

Are you working endlessly for something with an expiration date?

At Your Word

It is by faith we understand that the whole world was made by
God's command so what we see was made by something
that cannot be seen.

HEBREWS 11:3 NCV

God, commanding the world into existence is something
I can't wrap my mind around. You just spoke and it was. If
only words were used in the creation of the whole world,
you can do anything. But with all that power, you gave
me free will. Eve ate the fruit because she chose the fruit.
I can choose you or I can choose sin.

Each day your power works around me and for me. You
are guarding me and guiding me, but I also have the
opportunity to choose to believe in your power and walk
by faith. That is so amazing to me, Lord, that you would
give me such power like that. Today I choose you and I
choose to have faith in your almighty power that is found
in your Word and all around me.

Do you believe that God's power still speaks?

AF

Right or Left

Whether you turn to the right or to the left,
your ears will hear a voice behind you, saying,
"This is the way; walk in it."
Isaiah 30:21 niv

God, it's easier to trust the thing I know to guide me.
I know social media and what's popular. I can follow
those trends and commit to working toward growing in
popularity. The voice of achievement calls me to work
consistently for approval by succeeding. I follow these
other meaningless goals because I can see them and I
know them.

But I want to know you, Lord. I want to trust you and
follow you. I can't see, touch, and hear you like these
other types of leaders in my life, but I have faith that you
know my path better than anything else.

Do you trust God to lead you?

AF

Free to Serve

As God's loving servants, you should live in complete freedom,
but never use your freedom as a cover-up for evil.
1 PETER 2:16 TPT

God, in your Word you say you bless those who follow your will. Often I choose to obey because I am waiting for the blessings in return. I am not serving and loving from the heart, but for selfish motives.

Lord, you gladly bless me when I listen to you and choose your path, but how much more will you bless me when I am obeying from a loyal heart and not an ambitious one. I choose to serve you continually because you are good to me.

Do you follow God out of the joy of the freedom he gives or out of obligation?

AF

Indescribable Gift

Thanks be to God for his indescribable gift!
2 Corinthians 9:15 nkjv

God, I am a part of a family of believers. There is nothing that can separate me or them from your love. I need nothing but to believe in you because believing in you provides me with endless blessings.

Jesus, you gave your life for me, and each day I receive blessings because of your sacrifice. I have a family and friends who love me, a school where I can learn, jobs available to me, and a God who has my best interests at heart. There is nothing more that I need. I thank you for this gift of love and mercy you give continuously.

What is the best gift you have ever received?

No More Tears

"He will wipe every tear from their eyes,
and there will be no more death or sorrow or crying or pain.
All these things are gone forever."
REVELATION 21:4 NLT

God, happiness is fleeting but joy is eternal. You never say that you promise happiness because happiness is only for good moments. Joy is choosing to be positive even in negative circumstances. There is a day coming when I can live in endless joy with you in heaven.

While I am still living in the world surrounded by troubles and trials, I choose to receive your joy, Father. When I cry, am in pain, or lose a loved one, I know that these feelings are short lived because they won't be present in eternity. Only joy and peace will reign forever. Today, I will look at each circumstance through your lens, seeing the positive in every situation.

Can you imagine a life without sorrow?

AF

Hypocrisy

"You hypocrite! First, take the wood out of your own eye.
Then you will see clearly to take the dust out of your friend's eye."
MATTHEW 7:5 NCV

God, it's easier to think that other people are in the wrong because I don't see behind the scenes. I know what circumstances lead me to fall into sin so I have more grace for myself, but I can never fully understand what happened in another person's life to make them the way they are or causes them to act the way they do.

Lord, you know everything about me and you choose to give me grace. In the same way, I choose to show love to everyone even if my first reaction might be to judge them for their sin.

Are you quick to judge others or to extend grace?

Take Me Deeper

Let us stop going over the basic teachings about Christ again and again. Let us go on instead and become mature in our understanding. Surely we don't need to start again with the fundamental importance of repenting from evil deeds and placing our faith in God.

HEBREWS 6:1 NLT

God, Christianity can often be mistaken for a lifestyle instead of what it is—a relationship with you. A relationship can't develop if there is no desire to dig deeper into discovering more about the other person. In the same way, my faith can't grow unless I dig deeper into understanding the Bible and who you are.

I choose to dig deeper today and press into your love, Lord. You hold nothing back from me but wait patiently for me to run after you. I set aside unhealthy relationships that are holding me back in my faith and habits that don't please you. I want nothing holding me back as I give everything for you today.

Have you become comfortable in your faith, or is there a hunger for more?

AF

Not Slow

The Lord is not slow about His promise, as some count slowness,
but is patient toward you, not wishing for any to perish
but for all to come to repentance.
2 PETER 3:9 NASB

God, I expect certain things out of life that were never promised to me. Those things aren't fulfilled by you unless it is a part of your plan. I shouldn't sit here and demand to have what I want when you already bless me with all I need.

Father, there are things on my heart that I desire for my future and you know what they are. I believe you can do all things and nothing is impossible with you. Therefore, I give you all that I desire and wait patiently for when you bring them into my life. Today I pray you would give me a grateful heart so I can be content with what I have instead of reaching for what I don't.

Have you become discouraged in waiting on God's promise?

Peace on Earth

"Glory to God in the highest,
and on earth peace among those with whom he is pleased!"
LUKE 2:14 ESV

God, in the back of my mind I sometimes think that I am not worthy of your love. How can I ask for peace when I put myself in bad situations and let myself succumb to sin? Peace is not just for the good Christian because no one is truly good all the time. Peace is offered to anyone who believes and I believe.

Jesus, I believe you love me and you can overcome my worries and anxieties. I have no fear of today or tomorrow because you are by my side guiding me through the trials.

What worries and anxieties can you invite the peace of God into?

AF

Hasty Plans

The plans of the diligent lead surely to plenty,
But those of everyone who is hasty, surely to poverty.
PROVERBS 21:5 NKJV

God, I know that my plans are never better than your plans, but I don't always know what your plans are. I pray for guidance, but you answer in your own timing. Please send me people who can counsel me. I will continue to come to you in prayer for your guidance but also need people who can speak wisdom into my life.

Lord, help me to hear these words of wisdom whether they are from a friend, parent, or mentor, and apply it to my life. I seek your will above my will today and every other day.

Have you gotten counsel about the plans you're working toward?

AF

Doing My Thing

Each one of us has a body with many parts,
and these parts all have different uses.
In the same way, we are many,
but in Christ we are all one body.
Each one is a part of that body,
and each part belongs to all the other parts.

ROMANS 12:4-5 NCV

God, you created me to be unique—one of a kind. There is no other person on this earth that is like me. My life experiences, personality, talents, and flaws all make me unique. I have strengths that others don't, and I want to use these strengths to help people.

I don't want to serve myself by becoming independent from everyone but instead use my uniqueness to serve the people around me, Lord. Show me how to serve people today with the gifts that you have given me. Aspects of who I am are not meant to be hidden but used for your good purpose.

How do your gifts strengthen and serve others?

AF

Harder Tests

Do not be surprised at the fiery ordeal among you, which comes upon you for your testing, as though some strange thing were happening to you; but to the degree that you share the sufferings of Christ, keep on rejoicing, so that at the revelation of His glory you may also rejoice and be overjoyed.

1 Peter 4:12-13 nasb

God, I will not complain when trials arise. My life compared to so many others around the world is simple and blessed. If you can overcome death, disease, poverty, depression, and every other evil thing, what do I have to fear?

Trials will arise in my life but they are only there to strengthen my faith, Lord. You don't cast burdens upon me to break me down but you promise to build me up. You overcame death on the cross so I could live this joyful, blessed life. If I don't have to fear death because I have a life in eternity, then any test I face today is only going to bring me closer to you.

When you face trials, do you believe that God is with you?

AF

Just that Much

Christ proved God's passionate love for us by dying in our place while we were still lost and ungodly!
ROMANS 5:8 TPT

God, by loving me you wash me of all my sin. I have no weakness that you can't strengthen. Fear and doubt may surround me but you are with me. Your love surrounds me and watches over me. All my weaknesses are of this world, but you say that they won't carry with me into eternity.

While I am here, you promise to guard and protect me. When trials I face are stronger than my will to do what's right, I pray you would strengthen my will to persevere. Nothing good comes without trials and my faith won't grow without some defeats along the way. Today, I rest on you, the rock of my faith that strengthens me even in my weakest moments.

Do you believe that God's love is greater than your biggest weakness?

AF

Before this Moment

For every matter there is a time and judgment,
Though the misery of man increases greatly.
ECCLESIASTES 8:6 NKJV

God, what makes me anxious is not knowing. Not knowing what my career will be, who I will marry, where I should live, who to be friends with, and so on. I want to have some kind of idea or plan for my life so I can feel like I'm in control.

You have control over everything, God. You guard the future so my faith is in you and not my own understanding. I must trust that you have a plan for me and be patient for the things I desire. There is no timing that is better than your timing. I trust that whatever happens today is part of your plan and I wait patiently for the things of the future.

Are you impatient with God's timing in an area of your life?

Slow Down

The wise see danger ahead and avoid it,
but fools keep going and get into trouble.
PROVERBS 27:12 NCV

God, I'll go long periods without spending time with you. Then when I remember how important my faith is, I set high expectations of what I should do to get back on track with my faith. But there is no making up for lost time with you.

Father, I need to slow down and realize that reading my Bible everyday isn't the only way I can grow my faith. Talking to you when I am waiting in line or worshiping in my car are important ways I can rest in your presence as well. Even when I am busy, I will find moments when I can pause and reflect on all the good things you have given me and rest in your love.

Have you been going nonstop, or are you making room for reflection and rest?

AF

Bold and Yielding

Going a little farther, he fell on the ground and prayed that, if it were possible, the hour might pass from him. And he said, "Abba, Father, all things are possible for you. Remove this cup from me. Yet not what I will, but what you will."

MARK 14:35-36 ESV

God, I sometimes keep what's really on my mind to myself. I pray with an absent mind, putting little of my heart into it. I think that sometimes feels safer. You say I should pour out my every desire, big and small.

When I have problems that are small or I think that what I have to pray about isn't worthy of your time, I keep it to myself. You want me to come to you with everything through prayer. Lord, I know you hear my prayers and you care about me. I pour my heart out to you because you will guard and protect me.

Have you poured your heart out to the Lord honestly lately?

Shared Comfort

*That we may be able to comfort those who are in any trouble,
with the comfort with which we ourselves are comforted by God.*
2 CORINTHIANS 1:4 NKJV

God, I often focus on how you can help me when I pray.
Prayer isn't meant for my own life but for others in need
too. All around me there are people who need your help
and guidance. From my family and friends to complete
strangers, there are endless amounts of people who
need prayer. How selfish of me to focus on my own
problems when others have far worse situations than I
do.

I pray for those who are hurting around me, people who
need your love. Whether Christian or not these people
need you, Lord. Protect and provide for them today and
touch them with your love.

Who is hurting around you that you can offer comfort to?

AF

Finishing

"I know that You can do all things,
And that no plan is impossible for you."
JOB 42:2 NASB

God, giving my all to everything I do can be tiresome.
What keeps me driven is the goal of success, but that
goal is fleeting. When I realize that there is no real
purpose to worldly success I become daunted by the
tasks at hand and procrastinate everything in life. I need
to have a new goal that is sustaining to keep me on track
with my tasks.

I could give up on getting good grades, keeping a
healthy diet, reading my Bible in the morning, or living
like you lived, Jesus, if my only goal was success. My
new goal is to please you. You want me to try my best at
everything I do, and I know that blessings come with hard
work from a good heart. So, I choose to work hard today
because you strengthen my will to persevere.

What have you been ready to give up on that God can
strengthen you to persevere in?

AF.

Blessed Words

A time to tear, and a time to sew;
a time to keep silence, and a time to speak.
ECCLESIASTES 3:7 ESV

God, always speaking my mind and being the center of attention are things that are glorified by society. People who have the best witty remarks or can trash talk anyone on the spot are confident and well respected. The people who have few words and only speak life are not always recognized. However, you recognize people for their good hearts.

I want to be wise with my words and only speak when it glorifies you, Lord. I can't praise and worship you and then curse and gossip out of the same mouth. If I am going to truly honor you with my words in worship and in prayer, I must also honor you when I am speaking with friends. When I begin to say things that are not right in your eyes, set off warning bells in my heart and mind so I reconsider my words and choose to speak life.

Do you pause to consider your words before you say them?

AF

Cannot Lose

In all these things we are more than conquerors through Him
who loved us. For I am persuaded that neither death nor life, nor
angels nor principalities nor powers, nor things present nor things
to come, nor height nor depth, nor any other created thing, shall
be able to separate us from the love of God which is in Christ
Jesus our Lord.
ROMANS 8:37-39 NKJV

God, what if I am not enough? Not pretty enough, smart
enough, kind enough, or strong enough? I can't be
everything people expect. When I meet new people and
they like me, I become paranoid that once they get to
really know me they won't like me as much. My goofiness
or imperfections might scare them away. But I am fully
loved by you.

Father, people have unrealistic expectations for me, but
you expect nothing. On my worst days or my best days,
you love me the same. When the fear of being imperfect
or of failing creeps into my mind, I will remember your
love and walk in confidence.

What situations can you carry the confidence of God's
love into today?

AF

Extravagant Love

A child has been born to us; God has given a son to us.
He will be responsible for leading the people.
His name will be Wonderful Counselor, Powerful God,
Father Who Lives Forever, Prince of Peace.
ISAIAH 9:6 NCV

Jesus, my life seems to be my own, but it is not just my own. It belongs to you, the Prince of Peace, Wonderful Counselor. I try to rely on my own strength to get me through the day. When night comes, I am exhausted and depressed. I didn't invite you into every area of my life.

Then there are times when I pray to you throughout the day, Lord. Those days are the best days. All the worries, troubles, anxieties, and conflicts that arise are easily overcome when I have you by my side. Today, I invite you into every moment so that joy and peace fill and surround me.

What area can you invite the Prince of Peace into today?

AF

Christmas Gift

"Today in the town of David a Savior has been born to you; he is the Messiah, the Lord."
LUKE 2:11 NIV

God, the birth of your Son, Jesus, was the beginning of the atonement for my sins. Without him becoming a man, there could be no crucifixion and I would be dead in my sin.

Jesus, your birth was so important because it led to your sacrifice on the cross, and that means when I sin, I am forgiven. The keys of death were taken away from the devil and by doing so, you granted me life with you forever. There is no greater sacrifice than what you made for all people. Thank you for being born and becoming the Savior of the world.

Why is the birth of Jesus significant to remember and celebrate?

AF

Power Infused

I have saved these most important truths for last:
Be supernaturally infused with strength through your life-union
with the Lord Jesus. Stand victorious with the force of his
explosive power flowing in and through you.
EPHESIANS 6:10 TPT

God, you created the whole universe and your power
is greater than any other. Why do I doubt your power to
change lives? You say that you hear all my prayers, but
that doesn't mean you'll grant my every wish. By saying
no or answering in ways that are better than my ways,
you show how great your power really is.

I think I know what is best, Lord, but you see all things
and work them together for my good. I am confident that
your power is wiser and more gracious than my will. I
trust that you know best and can do all things, today and
every day.

Are you confident of God's power to change lives?

AF

Be Fruitful

Be careful how you walk, not as unwise people but as wise,
making the most of your time, because the days are evil.
EPHESIANS 5:15-16 NASB

God, I let myself be distracted. I blame social media, friends, work, school, and sports for taking up too much time, but there is always time for you. I choose to spend time scrolling through apps and texting friends, but I don't choose reading my Bible as often.

I want to pick what is most worthy of my time, and what is more worthy than you, Lord? I set aside the distractions in my life and choose to ignore the excuses. Today I will spend my time in prayer and the Word because nothing could benefit me more than a strong relationship with you.

How are you using your time?

AF

Never Forgotten

"Can a woman forget the baby she nurses?
Can she feel no kindness for the child to which she gave birth?
Even if she could forget her children, I will not forget you."
ISAIAH 49:15 NCV

God, I search for approval and love in all the wrong places. Relationships are never going to fully satisfy me. The only relationship that is one hundred percent fulfilling is my relationship with you.

Lord, your love surrounds me and works in me to mend any brokenness from past relationships. Friends will let me down, but your love will be with me for eternity. I am completely satisfied with your love and your love alone.

Do you believe that God loves you completely, just as you are in this moment?

AF

Increased Humility

Humble yourselves under the mighty power of God,
and at the right time he will lift you up in honor.
1 PETER 5:6 NLT

God, I want to be truly known and loved for who I am.
When I seek this kind of approval from others, I work for
success and status to gain acceptance. But you already
know me. You created me in my mother's womb and you
know my every thought.

There is no reason for me to strive for approval from the
world because I already have your approval and love,
Jesus. Thank you for loving me through all my downfalls.
I submit all my worries, selfish ambitions, and insecurities
to you. Being humble doesn't mean I am weak; rather,
that I put others before myself in the same way you did. I
choose to do that today and every other day.

What can you submit to God that you have been striving
for others to see?

AF

Awe Inspired

"His mercy extends to those who fear him,
from generation to generation."
LUKE 1:50 NIV

God, your existence makes me stop in my tracks. I'm surrounded by a reality that only exists because of your intricate handiwork. You invented all science! You decided my eye color! Your greatness is unfathomable, and you still devote time to me. I'm so thankful that you love me. When you could have been distant, you decided to want relationship with your creation. You are so wonderful.

My soul praises you, mighty King! I am so in awe of you. You raise up the weak and bring down the strong, and every action you take is exactly correct—down to the last detail. Thank you for making me and pouring out your love on me every day. Give me a new revelation of what you're doing on earth and in heaven. Increase my awareness of your presence.

Have you considered all the blessings of God in your life lately?

EHS

Journey Together

The LORD will fulfill his purpose for me;
your steadfast love, O LORD, endures forever.
Do not forsake the work of your hands.
PSALM 138:8 ESV

God, the journey of life has so many ups and downs. When the problems of life are suffocating, you are my breath of fresh air. Thank you for guiding me through this year and teaching me more about your Spirit.

There is nothing I need more in this next year than to continue to walk in my faith. If I lost everything but still had you, I would have enough. You have blessed me abundantly and continue to amaze me with your grace. As the new year begins, give me a renewed desire to pursue you wholeheartedly.

When you look at the journey of your life so far, where do you see God's hand moving you?

AF